COLLABORATIVE-APPRENTICESHIP LEARNING

LANGUAGE AND THINKING ACROSS THE CURRICULUM, K–12

D0140248

COLLABORATIVE-APPRENTICESHIP LEARNING

LANGUAGE AND THINKING ACROSS THE CURRICULUM, K–12

ANN SHEA BAYER

University of Hawaii at Manoa

Mayfield Publishing Company

Mountain View, California
London • Toronto

Library of Congress Cataloging-in-Publication Data

Bayer, Ann Shea.
  Collaborative-apprenticeship learning : language and thinking
  across the curriculum, K–12 / Ann Shea Bayer.
      p.   cm.
  Includes bibliographical references.
  ISBN 0-87484-882-2
  1. Education—Experimental methods. 2. Language arts—Correlation
  with content subjects. 3. Teacher-student relationships.
  4. Teaching—Vocational guidance.   I. Title
LB1027.3.B39   1990
428'.007—dc20   89-29786
                                                                    CIP

Manufactured in the United States of America
10 9 8 7 6 5 4 3 2 1

Mayfield Publishing Company
1240 Villa Street
Mountain View, California 94041

Sponsoring editors, Alden Paine and Franklin C. Graham; managing editor, Linda Toy; production editor, Carol Zafiropoulos; manuscript editor, Loralee Windsor; text and cover designer, Jeanne M. Schreiber; production artist, Jean Mailander. The text was set in 10/12 1/2 Palatino and printed on 50# Glatfelter Spring Forge by Thomson-Shore.

CONTENTS

v

PREFACE

This book is designed for students who are preparing to enter the teaching profession, as well as for experienced teachers who are looking for some assistance in improving student language and thinking competencies.

Two major educational concerns today are (1) the language and thinking competencies of our students and (2) the quality of teaching at all levels in our schools. Responses to these concerns have produced a number of suggestions for change. The most promising of these suggestions reflect new knowledge about language and learning: that is, learners engaged in using language as a tool for learning not only increase their understanding of course content but also become more competent language users. Many books and journal articles exist on such topics as "writing across the curriculum," "using learning logs in the elementary classroom," "writing response groups in history classes," "talk as a tool for learning," and "whole language classrooms."

The new focus on giving students opportunities to use language as a tool for learning goes hand in hand with discussion of how active student participation changes traditional teacher-student roles. The teacher is typically the primary language user in the classroom, asking the questions, delivering the lecture, and evaluating students' responses. It is not surprising that a second body of texts and journal articles is appearing on such topics as "the teacher as learner," "collaborative learning," and "the teacher as coach." These two bodies of work reflect a new teaching paradigm that places student language and thinking at center stage with the teacher as guide.

Two examples of this new teaching paradigm in practice are elementary level and secondary classrooms committed to a whole language approach and classrooms influenced by the National Writing Project or the writing across the curriculum movement. Although traditional teaching practices continue to dominate our schools, these classrooms are growing in number.

Change can be difficult to begin and sustain. This book adds a tool for change by providing teachers with a new teaching model. The model relies on a handful of language and learning principles to guide teaching practices. It shows teachers how they can begin to change within their current situations and how student successes encourage and sustain change. The model is called Collaborative-Apprenticeship Learning (CAL) because one of its underlying principles is L. S. Vygotsky's idea that learning is primarily social. Students need opportunities to collaborate with each other, as well as with the teacher, to learn and gain expertise within a particular field, just as apprentices do outside school.

Because of its across-the-curriculum focus this book is as appropriate for content area teachers as for those who are primarily involved in English education and language arts.

Novice teachers in preservice programs can use the model to help them understand why and how certain strategies promote both language and thinking. They can use the model to plan and evaluate their classroom observations, tutoring, student-teaching, and internships. Experienced teachers can use the model as a guide for rethinking teacher-student roles. Both groups can look for connections between their attempts at change and the experience of the K–12 teachers amply quoted throughout the book.

The introduction sets the stage by describing the author's personal journey away from traditional teaching. It is one teacher's story that mirrors the development of a new paradigm in education. The main body of the work contains three parts. Part I emphasizes first the reasons for changing teaching models in a theoretical chapter (Chapter 1) and then sets forth the model itself (Chapter 2). Part II (Chapters 3–4) illustrates the use of the model in the author's classes and is set up so teachers can look for connections with their own K–12 teaching situations.

The first chapters of Part III (Chapters 5–6) contain the experiences of teachers from kindergarten through college who have used this model, including what went wrong and how they solved problems. The last chapter (Chapter 7) expands on the issues that come up inside and outside the classroom when teachers are involved in change. Some teachers may prefer to read Parts I and III first, returning to the middle section for a more detailed account of collaborative-apprenticeship learning in one classroom.

ACKNOWLEDGMENTS

Writing this book reminded me once again of the role that collaboration plays in my work. Heartfelt thanks go to the following teachers who allowed me to include their "voices": Haunani Abdul, Kathleen Andrasick, Haunani Bernardino, Elizabeth Borengasser, Marilyn Broadbent, Lori Cambra, Linda Crockett, Craig Doyle, Tony Lee, Roman Leverenz, Forrest Lum, Joyce Miyamoto, Karen Mukai, Sue Nishikawa, Beverly Sandobal, Liane Sato, Anna Sumida, Jean Sumiye, Stanford Sundlie, Ann Thomas, Cissy Tucker, Sharon Vincent, Lianne Seu Wong, Sandi Wong, and Renee Young. It is difficult to try out new ideas in private let alone in the public arena. Their courage and sense of professionalism is impressive.

This book not only reflects my own and my K–12 colleagues' teaching experiences but also is shaped by an analysis of the teaching-learning processes that I was able to do thanks to the support of the NCTE Research Foundation and the University of Hawaii. I appreciate their faith in me.

My own colleagues at the University of Hawaii, especially Joy Marsella and Betsy Brandt, prodded, questioned, and listened as I struggled with the early drafts. Members of the Hawaii Research on Thinking Project (HaRT), Alison Adams, Betsy Brandt, Karen Watson-Gegeo, Suzanne Jacobs, and Paula Levin, helped me shape the theoretical perspective underlying the CAL model.

I would also like to extend my appreciation to the following reviewers of the text for their many excellent suggestions: Kim Cooley, University of California at San Diego; Harvey Daniels, National College of Education; Sarah Hudelson, Arizona State University; Paula Levin, University of California at San Diego; Grace Nunn, Eastern Illinois University; and Gordon Pradl, New York University.

Needless to say, a book would not exist today if I didn't have editors who saw "something" in my rough drafts. I cannot thank Alden Paine enough. Supportive from the beginning, he guided me through the complex process leading to publication with patience, intelligence, and humor. Frank Graham's thoughtful and insightful feedback provided me with the direction I needed for revision. Both editors worked to help me fulfill my intentions. Indeed, everyone I worked with at Mayfield was supportive and patient. Thank you Tom Broadbent, Gwen Larson, John Harpster, Carol Zafiropoulos, Pam Trainer, and Loralee Windsor.

And to Myrna Nakasato, who typed and retyped this manuscript during evenings and weekends, "Mahalo."

To
my Shea family

INTRODUCTION

It was a remedial reading class of ninth graders, fifteen boys. I can still remember some of their names: Michael, Daryl, William. I had no previous experience teaching reading. I had been an American history major, and this was my second teaching job. For some time I had worried about that first day, thinking "What should I do?" Of course I relied on my own experiences as a student. The teacher asks the student to read aloud and listens for correct pronunciation. I asked Daryl to read a paragraph, and then each of the other boys took turns hesitantly, mumbling—until it was Michael's turn. Michael was quiet for what seemed like a very long time. We were all looking at him, and then he burst into tears. I remember thinking, "There is nothing that important about reading paragraphs aloud, especially if it causes students to cry." I said to the class, "From now on whenever we read to each other, I will ask only those who volunteer to read; if you do not volunteer you will not be called on." Now I had to come up with something else to do. Could I read to them? Maybe we could choose plays to read to each other? Maybe we could work with partners and read together? We tried these activities, and with the pressure off the students began to relax, and so did I.

That year was the beginning of my interest in language and learning. Unfortunately I had neither the knowledge nor the experience to trust my intuitive teaching strategies, especially when the district language arts consultant came to administer diagnostic tests to my students. She was a wonderfully kind individual, but I couldn't understand her when she talked to me about my students' reading. She said things like, "William appears to be having difficulty with serial reversals of consonant blends in the medial position of sequential ordering." I'd smile blankly, thinking, "If I'm really

1

going to be a reading specialist, I need to be able to talk like her." I decided then to go back to school and get a master's degree in reading.

Michael volunteered to read a play part in May. He and the other boys were congratulated by their other teachers for their improved reading, and I was off to learn "how to really teach reading."

My graduate program in 1970 was probably fairly typical. It provided no explicit theoretical basis for reading methods that I can recall. I learned to break the reading process into small bits and to teach the bits in a sequence; eventually the students would put the bits together and comprehension would take care of itself. There was no mention of writing in my program; no one thought about the interrelationships among the various language processes. I was a good student; I graduated talking like my former language arts consultant.

Shortly thereafter (1971) I was hired to chair and redesign a middle school reading program. No problem. I instituted standardized group testing, individual diagnostic testing, and individualized prescription lesson plans. I consulted with teachers, indicating which of their students had "serial reversals, minimal auditory discrimination, and perceptual difficulties." I didn't mention comprehension or writing. I walked the halls briskly, carrying clipboards and looking efficient. But in my own remedial classes, I was bored. I sensed that my students, working away in their individualized prescription lesson plans, were also bored. Something was not working. My students were no more interested in reading at the end of the year than they were at the beginning.

Fortunately I worked with more experienced colleagues. One day one of these colleagues came up to me. I was afraid of Margaret who was smart and aggressive. She said, "I fail to see the purpose of testing students on syllabication. Why are you doing that to improve reading comprehension?" No one had ever asked me *why* I was doing what I was doing before. I thought about her question for several days but I had no good answer. Margaret continued to ask me, "why this and why that." I could see she was onto something, so I invited her to discuss with me and the other reading faculty "why" we had the program we did and to help us consider changes. This was the beginning of our professional collaboration in a study group that continued for several years. It was also the beginning of our involvement in a paradigm shift, although we were not conscious of that at the time.

One of the first questions we raised in our study group was "What is the purpose of reading instruction?" We agreed that it was to help students construct meaning from reading material. What followed was the question, "How can we best use our class time to do this?" Again we agreed that students needed time for silent reading of books in which they had an interest. That was what we adults did, we reasoned. We agreed that taped books would be available to anyone needing assistance, thereby eliminating the need for homogeneous reading groups; skills would be taught within the context of the students' reading material, when needed (Bayer 1977).

Allowing our students to select their own reading materials increased their chances of reading for meaning because they would choose books on topics about which they had enough background knowledge to comprehend the text at some level and yet learn something new. This meaning-centered approach to reading reflected the early stages of the whole language curriculum (Goodman 1986), in which students are now encouraged to use reading, talking, and writing for real purposes.

In 1978, I attended the Bay Area Writing Project Summer Institute. Participation in that institute not only changed my self-image as a writer but also led to my search for reading and writing connections. In the literature on writing development I began to discover a paradigm shift that was theoretically consistent with what was happening in reading. Writing seemed to develop best when students wrote and revised their writing pieces for real purposes and real audiences.

Back I went to graduate school to investigate the role that talk plays in learning. I was becoming uncomfortable with trying to keep the language processes separated because it was increasingly clear to me that we need all the processes to help us make sense out of the world. But I was not thinking much about the social milieu in which language and learning takes place. Instead I was focusing on the integration of the language processes (reading, writing, talking, listening) and the development of these processes by using language as a tool for learning across the curriculum. I took for granted the social context in which all of this took place. For example, it did not occur to me that the writing project staff development model exemplifies collaborative learning with its focus on writing groups and peer teaching.

But now I'm back in the classroom. The students are older (university), but they have the same problems in principle. They still need to make connections between new ideas and prior knowledge; they still use language as a tool for learning.

Unlike the middle school reading program, this teaching situation introduces specific bodies of knowledge into the course. In the middle school reading classes the focus was on a few instructional strategies that students could use to help them comprehend whatever materials they chose to read. For the majority of the instructional time the students silently read self-selected materials.

In the courses I currently teach I want my students to examine both instructional strategies and specific bodies of knowledge related to the discipline of English education. These courses resemble content-area courses like American literature or East Asian history classes.

Valid principles underlying good teaching-learning processes remain the same in either type of class. What changes is the degree of guidance novice students might need for content-specific tasks. Because some students enter a particular content area with insufficient knowledge to understand the discipline's major concepts, it is difficult for them to study these topics independently. I found myself faced with the question of what strategies would help students make connections between the new ideas and their background knowledge. And it was this dilemma that made me conscious of the social milieu in which teaching-learning processes occur.

Examining the social contexts in which learning takes place led me to rethink the work of Vygotsky (1978; 1962). The following chapter outlines Vygotsky's concept of the social origins of learning as the central principle from which other language and learning principles operate.

PART ONE

RATIONALE

This part provides the theoretical foundation for collaborative-apprenticeship learning (CAL). It also introduces the application of this model to various teaching contexts across the curriculum.

1

VYGOTSKY
REVISITED

SOCIAL ORIGINS
OF LEARNING

Up to the time I began teaching at university level, the major language and learning principles that had guided my teaching included:

1. Students have to make connections between new ideas discussed in class and their prior knowledge.
2. Students can use language to help them make these connections, that is, they can use language as a tool for learning.
3. Students' language and thinking competencies develop with regular use in meaningful problem-solving tasks.

I wasn't sure how to help my university students get started making connections. They were novices within this discipline of English language education. Having them self-select books to read, the major strategy I used in the middle school reading program, seemed to leave too big a gap between the ideas they were reading about and their background knowledge.

While experimenting with classroom practices myself, I became especially interested in observing the interactions of students working in small groups to solve some meaningful task. This made me conscious of the whole issue of the social milieu in which we learn. Vygotsky's (1978) belief in the social origins of learning began to make more sense to me as I observed what was happening in my classroom. Vygotsky argued that "every function of the child's cultural development appears twice: on the social level, and later, on the individual level; first, between people (interpsychological), and then inside the child (intrapsychological) . . . all the higher functions originate as actual relations between human beings" (1978).

This means that individuals help each other construct meaning, which is eventually internalized by the individuals. This process can be readily seen in dialogue. In the following excerpt from an earlier case study (Bayer 1986) Alice, a high school anthropology teacher, is trying to help Marion, a home economics teacher, understand the meaning of the technical phrase, *reconstructed knowledge*:

Marion: . . . and you're saying it isn't "knowledge" until . . .

Alice: You see they have *knowledge* in half quotes here, and I wondered if they [the authors] were saying that it wasn't "knowledge" *really* until it was reconstructed . . . you see?

Marion: I don't understand that.

Alice: Alright. Suppose you give your recipe and *tell* how to cook something versus having a youngster cook it and taste it and see it—making it your own in some way . . . .

Marion: Understandable! OK! That would be like the commercial I've been hearing everyday . . . .

When Marion didn't understand Alice's first explanation, Alice tried again. This time she considered Marion's frame of reference as a cooking teacher by using an example to which Marion could relate. Apparently Marion was then able to make a connection between the idea of "reconstructed knowledge" and what she knew about teaching cooking. She was, at least in part, internalizing what had previously existed in dialogue between Alice and her.

This does not mean that Marion came away from this experience thinking just like Alice. Marion did not copy or imitate Alice's thinking; she had to make sense out of the discussion the best way that she could given her own background knowledge.

Bruner supports this social interactive perspective and notes that developmental psychologists have recently given "more weight to interaction with others, and to the use of language, in the growth of concepts and the developing structure of the mind" (1987, 8). He suggests that a child's development must be mediated through interaction with others.

APPRENTICESHIPS

How might learners engage in joint activities to promote conceptual development? Vygotsky postulated that an expert (or more knowledgeable peer) initially guides a learner's (novice) activity; gradually the two begin to share the problem-solving functions, with the novice taking the initiative and the expert peer correcting and guiding when she or he falters. Finally the expert peer cedes control and acts as a supportive audience (Brown & Ferrara 1985).

Vygotsky further argued that engaging in these joint activities advances the novice's level of actual development. He suggests that a novice's boundaries lie between (1) his or her actual development, or what he or she can do independently; and (2) his or her potential development, or what he or she can do while participating with more capable others. Vygotsky calls this a learner's "zone of proximal development" (1978). (This concept will be abbreviated as *ZPD* throughout the rest of the text.)

The idea of someone with more expertise helping someone with less is so obvious in parent-child relationships. For example, at first parents or older siblings, feed babies and gradually the babies increasingly feed themselves until they can do it independently. Most of us can probably recall being either the novice or the expert in a similar apprenticeship process. Right now I'm still very much the novice in the computer world. I need the guidance of someone with more expertise until I can internalize what I need to know and the expert can "back away."

The question is, of course, whether this same apprenticeship process will work as a teaching-learning model in our educational settings across grade levels. I think it can. One of the first issues to consider is how to begin. In the parent-child apprenticeship, the mother and father know a great deal about their child's levels of actual development because of the intimacy of the home situation. Even in traditional apprenticeships outside the home, such as tailor and apprentice or artist and protégé, the one to one ratio helps the expert gain knowledge of the novice's abilities. In classrooms, however, the novices are likely to be strangers and the teacher-student ratio is not one to one but more likely one to thirty or one to seventy-five. How can a teacher determine the students' competencies?

SCAFFOLDING STRUCTURE

The scaffolding structure I developed addresses this question. As in other apprenticeship relationships, my relationship with adult students is more asymmetrical at the beginning of the year than at the end. During the first few weeks, I spend more time engaging students in joint activities designed to make public their knowledge and interest in topics and helping them build on what they already know. These joint activities are meant to give shape to Vygotsky's ZPD concept by beginning with the students' present levels of development and jointly working to expand the students' comprehension and knowledge.

I have borrowed Bruner's (1978) term *scaffolding* to mean guided participation in joint activities that help students assimilate new ideas. Let me give you an example of a typical scaffolding process early in the semester. (Remember that this early in the school year novice students generally do not have sufficient knowledge of content-area concepts to work without guidance. As students assimilate these concepts the apprenticeship process begins to look different. Just as when children have practiced riding a bicycle with the parent running alongside for support, the parent eventually lets go and the child rides independently, the teacher cedes control during the school year so the students can take the initiative more often.)

To begin with I have some ideas about what I consider to be the major concepts, and my students have questions they want answered. I ask my students to write what they already know about a very broad, core concept in this field, such as, "How do individuals learn something new?" All students have some ideas about learning; they can each make a response based on prior knowledge. This use of writing to elicit knowledge and experience is called focused freewriting (Elbow 1976; 1981). Unlike traditional techniques (such as pretests), which are used at the beginning of a new topic, the freewrite activity is formulated as a question related to the concept being introduced, but worded so that students can use whatever knowledge they have, including everyday knowledge from living within this culture. The students read their individual freewrites to peers in small groups, and group members listen for similarities and differences between their currently held beliefs. This begins to make public the individual student's knowledge about the concept. It also begins peer collaboration early in the semester as group members pool their knowledge. Even in this early part of the school year peers can act as experts for each other, which alleviates the pressure on one instructor trying to respond individually to each student.

The small groups share their current beliefs about the freewrite topic with the whole class, thus making the information public to everyone including the instructor. The instructor takes the role of more capable peer to make connections between the different group beliefs and provide a picture of what seem to be the students' current theories about the topic.

I use this shared knowledge of the class participants as an anchor for negotiating the meaning of new knowledge about topic x. Now we have a starting point, and as the instructor I move to build on the shared background knowledge.

I ask the students to look for confirmation of their individual and group beliefs in an upcoming activity. They are to note discrepancies between their current beliefs and the new information they generated by participating in the activity. Which of their beliefs were confirmed during the demonstration? Which were not? So the students are looking for the connections they can make between the new ideas presented in class and their prior knowledge. They are actively involved in constructing meaning.

These hands-on demonstrations early in the semester typically engage students in activities that tap into everyday experiences and are related in some way to the topic under discussion. For the topic "learning," for example, I give the students unnamed objects (such as a cherry pit remover). Each student has to guess what the object is and then write down what led him or her to that particular guess.

Again the students share their responses with the whole class, and the instructor places them within a categorical scheme reflecting the new concept. In the case of the unnamed cherry pit remover, as the individual students shared their guesses, I list them on the board. When asked why they made such guesses, students often say something about seeing something similar in their mechanic's garage or their doctor's office. When asked why the guesses were different for the same object, students typically state that their experiences have been different. At that point I connect these student statements to the concept that learners activate their related prior knowledge to help them make sense out of a new situation. (Note that specialized vocabulary is introduced by labeling the student-generated information.)

This process continues until all the student responses are placed in the categorical scheme, leaving the instructor to fill in the gaps. Thus it is possible to use this scaffolding structure to begin at the students' actual levels of development and help them expand their knowledge through guided participation.

LANGUAGE AND LEARNING PRINCIPLES

The ZPD processes embedded in this scaffolding structure led me to add a new language and learning principle to my repertoire of three listed at the beginning of the chapter.

4. Learners need opportunities to work collaboratively under expert guidance and with more knowledgeable peers within an apprenticeship process; novice learners increasingly assume more responsibility for their own learning.

This fourth principle provides the social processes needed for the first three.

In this apprenticeship teaching-learning model, students do not remain in the same asymmetrical relationship with their instructor throughout the school year. As they assimilate the early concepts, they can take more responsibility for their learning, increasingly relying on each other in collaborative peer groups and using the teacher as a resource. Indeed I prefer to use the term *collaborative-apprenticeship learning* (CAL) for the model I'm proposing to emphasize the role that collaboration with both peers and instructor plays in the teaching-learning process.

PEER COLLABORATION

Unfortunately peer collaboration is not yet a major social structure in our classrooms. As Goodlad (1983, 1984) found, the dominant classroom structure takes one of two forms: Either the teacher is in front of the room giving a lecture to the whole class, or students are working alone on assigned tasks with the instructor checking their individual progress. Given the growing body of knowledge supporting the concept of social learning, I suspect this picture will change.

How does work in small groups help students internalize new ideas? Peer interaction in a problem-solving process promotes cognitive development and the use of critical thinking strategies. Individual group members faced with conflicting viewpoints attempt to clarify, analyze, synthesize, speculate, and evaluate the conflicting points of view as they work their way toward resolution. Individual cognitive reorganization is induced by group cognitive conflict (Barnes & Todd 1978; Inagaki & Hatano 1977; Perret-Clermont 1980; Forman & Cazden 1985; Bruner 1987). Johnson and Johnson (1979) have had similar results in their work, which they call cooperative learning. Bruffee (1984) writes eloquently about collaborative learning with college students. Cognitive development occurs, then, through the incorporation of others' viewpoints into our own thought processes (Mead 1934). Parker and Goodkin conclude that if there is "no social interaction with others who offer us an expanded range of alternative viewpoints, no new viewpoints to incorporate into our thinking, [there can be] no intellectual development" (1987, 38).

The implication of this theoretical perspective is an argument for heterogeneous peer groups. We have a tradition of "tracking" students, placing them in homogeneous classes based on standardized test results. This practice has more disadvantages than advantages (Hallenan 1984; Cohen 1986). Being a "more capable peer" for a particular topic or procedure means the student has some related background knowledge or experiences regarding topic x that he or she can use to guide a peer with less background knowledge. Students' background experiences vary. The more varied the group the more likely someone in the group can be of assistance when the group is engaged in problem solving. The more varied the group the more likely differing points of view will be introduced. Diversity is enriching.

One example of how collaboration might advance an apprentice learner's actual development comes from a case study (Bayer 1986) in which a group of five teachers worked with a chairperson to reach a consensus about the use of writing across the curriculum. The teachers, who came from several schools, grade levels, and subject areas, had recently participated in writing workshops. They were in the process of building on their knowledge about using writing as a tool for learning; the chairperson was initially considered to be the "more capable other."

As a group they were grappling with fairly new concepts. In the first session the chairperson suggested possible agendas and clarified areas of confusion. By the second session the group members had begun to ask questions of each other and to attempt to negotiate a shared meaning for the concept under discussion. They often began a discussion of a new concept by talking about something from everyday life that was related to the more abstract concept being examined. When Alice, a high school anthropology teacher, for example, approached the topic "natural language development," she talked about her experiences with her grandson.

> This is a grandchild of superior ability—but from the time he was three, he has been allowed to spell any way without any kind of direction. He just turned seven and he gave his mother a book of fifteen poems. The spelling is never corrected, and he has the most interesting ideas . . . and you wonder if inside every child this kind of original thinking gets washed out because somebody says you spell it t-i-o-n and not s-h-u-n and so on (Bayer 1984, 196).

Alice's example served as a common referent for the topic "natural language development" that all the participants in the group could understand; all group members could enter into the task at this level. The chairperson then tried to connect this example from the learner's personal experiences to the concept under discussion.

From such a common beginning point these participants proceeded to negotiate shared meanings of the concept under discussion by clarifying, extending, and qualifying their own and each other's tentative hypotheses. Negotiating shared definitions typically leads the apprentices (and the more capable peers) to reorganize their schema. From a Vygotskian perspective, the individual has internalized what was generated within the social milieu.

This collaborative approach implies a willingness to negotiate meaning; it encourages students to explore their understanding of a topic without fear of being wrong. It promotes the risk taking necessary to move beyond the status quo (Wertsch 1985).

It is important to note that the more capable peer is not always the one assisting the apprentices; the roles are not that constant. An apprentice-learner, perhaps because he or she is bringing a fresh perspective to the topic, can also clarify, extend, and qualify the hypotheses generated by other group members (Bayer 1986; Inagaki 1981). Again, heterogeneous groups work best because group members with diverse prior experiences broaden the collective pool of knowledge that the group can use for problem solving.

This notion of the teacher or peers guiding an apprentice learner only until the apprentice can assume more responsibility is especially appealing compared to my experiences in traditional classrooms, where the teacher typically remains in control throughout the school year. Students in traditional classrooms are not assuming any more responsibility for school-related tasks at the end of the school year than they were at the beginning; they remain dependent learners.

LANGUAGE AS A
TOOL FOR THINKING

The role that language plays in learning is made explicit during this process because language is the mechanism through which the negotiation of meaning occurs. In these classrooms the students are the primary language users. Rather than listening to the teacher talk two-thirds of the time, these students have regular opportunities to talk, read, and write as they attempt to construct explanations that make sense to them.

Much of the language used is expressive. Expressive language in both speech and writing allows the learner to express freely thoughts, feelings, and opinions about a subject. It is relatively unstructured because it is used in circumstances in which the speaker (or writer) knows the audience and relies on their shared experiences for understanding (Barnes, Britton & Rosen 1975).

Expressive language is a beginning point for coming to terms with new ideas. For example, students who are collaborating with each other in small groups are likely to use expressive talk. It sounds a lot like informal conversation, but its importance should not be underestimated. Through this talk the learner can "shape his ideas, modify them by listening to others, question, plan, express doubt, difficulty and confusion, experiment with new language and feel free to be tentative and incomplete" (Barnes, Britton & Rosen 1975, 162).

Britton and his colleagues (1975) argue that expressive language is the basis for the development of student language and thinking. To fulfill our teachers' dreams of students adept in using specialized vocabularies and appropriate language conventions, our students must be able to wrestle with the ideas informally before having to shape their thinking and language for the public.

EXPRESSIVE TALK

In the following excerpts from a case study on the role of talk and learning (Bayer 1986) members of a collaborative problem-solving group begin their discussions by using expressive talk (Barnes (1976) uses the term *exploratory talk*). As they work out the meanings of the various concepts under discussion, however, their talk becomes less expressive and more formal and includes appropriate uses of specialized vocabulary.

In the second session of a group of five teachers working on the use of writing in K–12 curriculums, Alice is grappling with the role that audience plays. She says, "you can talk to a small circle, but if you wanna reach a group that isn't present . . . if your Grandma's here you can talk to her. If she lives somewhere else you might write her a letter every week . . . . " The example that Alice uses comes from everyday living experiences and her language is informal. She is exploring connections between what she has been reading and doing in the writing workshops related to the concept of audience and her personal experiences.

For two sessions the group worked to clarify and expand each other's thinking about this concept, but no one used the term until the fourth session, when Marion asked, "When you're talking about writing assignment to a specific audience, you're saying that when you're asking a student to write a paper, you're asking them to write a paper for a particular group of people?" When Marion uses the term *specific audience*, she defines it by using an example, and she asks her group members for support of her definition. This ongoing internalization of negotiated meanings for the concept of audience continued to be reflected in their dialogue. No longer did they rely exclusively on examples from everyday living; the term *audience* was now part of their discussions. Eventually they agreed that the following statements about audience represented their shared belief: "Every writing assignment must be directed to a specific audience, preferably one that is significant to the writer. Students need to learn to write for a variety of audiences."

This last statement no longer sounds like expressive talk. A shift has occurred in the group members' thinking, and this shift is reflected in their language. Britton and his colleagues (1975) calls this transactional language. This kind of language is typically needed for school-related tasks. Its purpose is to transact some business in the world, "to inform people . . . to advise or persuade or instruct people" (Barnes, Britton & Rosen 1975, 134). And that was the intent of this group—to persuade their colleagues that students needed to learn to write to various audiences. But first they had to make clear among themselves what each person understood about the concept of audience. They did so through expressive talk.

A note of caution: A group member's internalized notion of audience was not likely to be a carbon copy of the others'. Each member had to reformulate the socially constructed meaning for herself to internalize it. Each member needed to connect the concept to her own prior knowledge.

Roman, a novice high school history teacher, reflects on why he would consider using talk in his future classrooms:

> Talking in small groups facilitates and greatly enhances the learning process. The major benefits are two. One, using small group discussion enables each individual to become more at ease with . . . sharing his thoughts with others. It helps to make ideas more alive to the students; more personal. By making ideas relate to one another and expressing how these ideas make and do not

make sense, each student is making the ideas presented in his class his "own." By doing this the student will certainly retain the ideas and concepts presented to him. (I know, that's already more than two benefits and I have not gotten to my second yet.)

The "second" major benefit of small group discussions is that group members can create a type of collective consciousness that provides constant feedback and analysis of the ideas brought up in discussion. If the group has a supportive atmosphere, and criticizes ideas and positions in order to help one another, each individual in the group must certainly benefit. The power of four or five brains and different points of view is certainly greater than one. A small group discussion becomes an enriched intellectual environment.

EXPRESSIVE WRITING

It's not only expressive talk that learners use to negotiate meaning. Expressive writing is also a tool for learning. Like expressive talk, expressive writing gives the learner a vehicle for freely expressing thoughts about a subject. It is informal because the audience is the author or a reader who has shared much of the author's experiences within a given context.

Clarifying one's thinking is a major function of expressive writing. Expressive writing allows the learner

> to select and hold for closer contemplation aspects of his own experience which can be scanned for particular features—sorted into logical or chronological order, rearranged for his own satisfaction. . . . This process of personal selection, contemplation and differentiation is very important because it changes the writer . . . because now he has articulated a feeling or a thought or an attitude more clearly, or seen how a bit of his experience fits into the pattern which he is gradually building up for himself; in other words, he is more conscious than he was. It is these processes which can go on in writing which can make it so powerful in an educational sense (Martin 1984, 34–35).

While learners may initially use expressive writing to make themselves conscious of the connections they are making (or not making) between new ideas and their background knowledge, they can also use expressive writing to engage in collaborative activities with the instructor. For example, students can keep learning logs and share them with the teacher. The same strategies of clarifying, expanding, and qualifying ideas that occurs in collaborative small groups can occur in written communications between the teacher and the student, resulting in negotiated shared meanings for the given topic.

And just as the language of the members of a small group changes as they work through new ideas, written language changes as its author assimilates new concepts. Once again the language shifts from expressive to transactional. Not all expressive writing has to be transformed into transactional writing, of course; it depends on the author's purpose and audience.

Transactional writing is used to inform or persuade people of something. The more public audience is less likely to have shared the author's experiences. Instead of using the informal language that characterizes expressive writing, the authors try to portray their own reshaped thinking within the appropriate genres and conventions of a particular discipline. This helps make their messages explicit and increases the chances that they will be understood by readers of various background experiences.

The processes authors engage in to "shape" a text are commonly known as revision and editing. Later chapters describe how to assist students as they work through these processes. It is important to remember that students need opportunities to wrestle with new ideas in expressive writing before they attempt transactional pieces. Given such opportunities and some choice in topic selection, students will produce quality pieces "when internalized . . . social speech is reshaped, revised and edited to become a composition, a term paper, a dissertation" (Bruffee 1983, 168).

TEACHER AS COLLABORATOR

If the students are the primary users of language within the classroom, what is the teacher's role? I referred earlier to Goodlad's (1983, 1984) description of the teacher as one who is either in front of the room giving a lecture to the whole class or among the students checking on the progress of individuals working alone. Teachers in these roles do most of the talking and writing. The teacher is viewed as an expert transmitting knowledge to students, whose job it is to absorb this knowledge and give it back in the form of tests. This role of the teacher has been with us for some time; therefore I'll refer to this model as traditional.

Within the traditional teaching model, the instructor is usually looking for a predetermined right answer. The teacher judges every response according to how close it comes to that one correct answer.

Barnes (1976) proposes an alternative teaching role, that of collaborator. This role describes teachers who "perceive the teacher's task [as that of] setting up a dialogue in which the learner can reshape his knowledge through interaction with others" (Barnes 1976, 144). Barnes went on to hypothesize that the teacher's responses to student utterances particularly affect the kind of learning that takes place; nonjudgmental responses are more likely to facilitate learning.

A collaborator is likely to try to withhold judgment to see what knowledge the students already have about the topic and to try to build on that knowledge by involving students in scaffolding activities, raising questions, and filling in gaps. Following student-generated knowledge means following the students' lead as they grapple tentatively with new ideas in small groups and in expressive writings. It means backing away as students are increasingly able to take responsibility for their own learning. Judgment day still comes, but now students have some say about which products will be evaluated to document what they have learned. The collaborator reflects Vygotsky's notion of novices working with an expert and more capable peers who initially guide the novice's activity; gradually the two begin to share the problem-solving functions and the novice takes the initiative. Finally the expert or peer cedes control and acts as a supportive audience.

The phrases *teacher as coach* and *teacher as facilitator* share the belief that students need to be active learners and not passive recipients of someone else's ideas. I appreciate the image raised by contrasting the traditional teacher and the sports coach. It is not the coach who is center stage during practice and games, it is the players.

In sum my educational journey over a twenty-year period has taken me from trying to make reading meaningful to Daryl, Michael, and William; to making connections between reading and writing, talking, and listening; to examining how these language processes can be used as tools for learning in our classrooms; and finally to investigating the social context in which language and learning take place and thereby discovering the powerful tool of collaboration.

In some of these experiences observing what was or wasn't working in my classroom prompted me to investigate possible theoretical explorations for the success or failure of certain practices; in other cases my involvement with theoretical models led me to try new classroom practices. The connection between theory and practice has become real to me.

What emerged from these experiences is a handful of language and learning principles that underlie collaborative-apprenticeship learning (CAL), a teaching model in which student language and thinking are central. The CAL model for teaching is described in Chapter 2.

2

COLLABORATIVE-
APPRENTICESHIP
LEARNING

USING THE MODEL
AS A GUIDE

I'm sure that many of the concepts discussed in the last chapter are not new to you. But teachers frequently tell me they sometimes feel overwhelmed by trying to piece together the ideas that they read about in professional journals and listen to in workshops. How do writing logs fit with small group discussion? What gets corrected? When is it appropriate for the teacher to back away? How can room be made for student intentions?

To novices it may seem a pretty big leap to incorporate some of these concepts. Experienced teachers whose only model of the teaching-learning process has been one of "covering the curriculum" may find it particularly difficult. But many realize that all is not well in their classrooms, and they are willing to consider change. The question for both novices and experienced teachers "in transition" is how to make the transition from the old curriculum-centered teaching model to collaborative-apprenticeship learning.

The model outlined in this chapter attempts to address that question, to integrate the various pieces of an alternative teaching-learning model. It also attempts to counter the "dumbing down" of our curriculum across the grades by proposing (as many others have done) that students need to be engaged in meaningful problem-solving tasks that demand varied language use and complex thinking strategies.

I propose this model as a scaffolding structure, something to be used as a temporary guide by both novices and experienced teachers. It is one way to begin to envision different roles, strategies, and content for teachers and students.

The model is based on four broad language and learning principles that reflect natural learning processes used by learners of all ages:

1. Learners are actively attempting to make sense out of their world, using their background knowledge as a frame of reference from which to generate hypotheses.

2. Working in collaboration with an instructor and peers within an apprenticeship process, learners construct knowledge beyond what they could do independently (ZPD).

3. Language is used as a tool for learning.

4. Students develop language and thinking competencies by using these processes regularly for meaningful problem-solving tasks.

To reflect these principles a teaching-learning model must view students as active learners trying to make sense out of school-related tasks; the more meaningful the task is to the student, the more motivated the student will be.

Instead of introducing new concepts from the teacher's frame of reference (as in a lecture), the instructor begins by eliciting what students already know about topic x. Helping students build on their knowledge involves providing opportunities for them to use familiar language and ideas and each other as resources while they engage in joint activities that illuminate the major concepts underlying topic x.

Having assimilated the basic concepts through collaborative-apprenticeship learning, students increasingly take the initiative for directing their own learning. They are encouraged to find answers to their own questions and to challenge the "received definitions" of existing knowledge. Students reshape and revise their thinking in preparation for sharing their viewpoints publicly in transactional pieces of writing, formal talks, or dramatic or musical presentations. The degree to which any student is involved in these processes will depend on age, context, and interest.

So the teaching-learning model that I have extrapolated from these four principles involves developing student language and thinking competencies within collaborative-apprenticeship learning. The process involves

- Starting with what students know
- Sharing that prior knowledge
- Building on that knowledge collaboratively
- Embedding language as a tool for learning throughout the process
- Increasingly supporting student initiative

The following chart is my attempt to make this model somewhat more explicit and to offer suggestions about how to implement it. Note that these are simply strategies that have worked for me. You may have other strategies that work as well or better within your teaching situation.

In the left-hand column of the following chart, I have outlined the collaborative-apprenticeship learning (CAL) model and some suggested teaching strategies. In the right-hand column, I have tried to make clear how students have regular opportunities to use language as a tool for learning as they engage in both individual and joint activities with their peers and instructor. The context for this process is an educational setting in which the learners are novices in a particular domain or content area.

CAL TEACHING MODEL, PART I

Sample Teaching-Learning Cycle	Students Using Language to Learn
Select major concept. Expand/modify to include student interests.	
Elicit student interest.	Students write/talk about discipline-related interests.
Start with what individual students know about concept.	Students write what they know.
How? Use focused freewriting; use brainstorming.	Students talk about what they know.
Make public what students know. How? Use small groups so students can pool their knowledge; small groups share knowledge with whole class. Collective prior knowledge becomes accessible to instructor and to each other.	Students collaborate with each other using expressive talk. Students look for confirmation of their current knowledge in scaffolding activities.
Build on what students know. How? Demonstrate the concept; model the concept/procedure. Place student-generated knowledge within conceptual framework.	Students engage in scaffolding activities.
Focus student reading. How? Students use what they already know and the concrete activities to make predictions about text material.	Students read to confirm own predictions.
Discover areas of student confusion. How? Use small groups so student can discuss what is or isn't clear.	Students collaborate with each other using expressive talk.
Use think/write logs so students can write what is or isn't clear.	Students collaborate with instructor using expressive writing.
Encourage application of ideas. How? Students independently (or in collaboration with others) engage in long-term projects of interest to them. Use writing response groups and peer research groups.	Students use writing, talking, listening, and reading as they engage in long-term projects.

Learners do not stay in the same place mentally. As they make tentative connections between new ideas and prior knowledge and internalize socially constructed ideas, they are better able to analyze, speculate, and evaluate course concepts. This is why students can take increasing responsibility for their own learning in the same way others take increasing responsibility in apprenticeships outside the school setting.

I typically spend the first third of a content-area class of novices engaging students in fairly concrete scaffolding activities. In the middle of the semester my students are working with their peers on long-term projects half the time and with me on new concepts half the time. During the final third of the course the students are working independently or with their peers almost exclusively, and I am used as a resource person and collaborator.

You can see this shift in the next chart. The students go as far as they can with their problem-solving groups, for example, asking for the teacher's assistance only when they get stuck. When the small groups share the results of their collaboration in a whole class discussion, the teacher may fill in gaps in the student's explanations, demonstrate a point using concrete examples; or raise questions to help students to continue their explorations.

In educational settings in which students already have some background knowledge in a particular discipline, the need for scaffolding activities decreases, and instructors and students can probably begin with processes (such as seminars) closer to the ones described in the chart on the opposite page.

In sum this model illustrates (1) a process that validates student-generated information as a beginning point for the examination of new ideas and (2) strategies that can be used to help students relate new ideas to their current knowledge. Having assimilated the basic concepts of the discipline students can begin to investigate further issues of interest, often critically analyzing these newly assimilated ideas and evaluating whether it makes sense to accept, reject, or modify the information that has been generated during the course. The framework reflects a dynamic teaching-learning process that changes over time and provides regular opportunities for students to use reading, writing, talking, and listening as tools for learning.

The model is not prescriptive; instructors at all levels and in various disciplines need to modify the process and suggested strategies according to the purposes, audiences, and conventions of their disciplines. Indeed this framework is a working model and will change over time. You will probably help change it if you try it out and note what seems to work for you and your students and what doesn't. It might be useful to meet with a colleague or study group to discuss the model and its implications for your teaching.

The remaining sections of this chapter address specific issues related to using the model in various teaching contexts.

CAL TEACHING MODEL, PART II

Sample Teaching-Learning Cycle	Students Using Language to Learn
Focus reading. How? Use focused freewrite; students read text looking for confirmation of current beliefs.	Students write what they know. Students read to confirm own predictions.
Students expand on what each knows. How? Use small groups so students can clarify and expand on each other's thinking about ideas in text. Share small group interpretations with whole class.	Students collaborate with each other using expressive talk.
Teacher fills in gaps. How? Provide missing connections, if any, in students' interpretations via concrete examples.	Teacher uses scaffolding activities for whole class instruction (if necessary).
Discover areas of student confusion. How? Use think/write logs so students can write what is or isn't clear.	Students collaborate with instructor by using expressive writing.
Encourage application of ideas. How? Students independently (or in collaboration with others) engage in long-term projects of interest to them.	Students use writing, talking, listening, and reading as they engage in long-term projects.

WHY "ACROSS THE GRADE LEVELS"?

Why address this book to novice and experienced teachers rather than looking for an audience at a particular grade level or content area? This idea came to me from my own teaching experience in various teaching assignments from elementary to university levels. Early in my teaching career I had adopted the attitude that if my students didn't know what I thought they should then something must have failed in the earlier grades. I was teaching seventh-grade social studies and assumed that the difficulties my students were having with language and learning must be due to inadequacies in their elementary education.

When I taught sixth-grade students, I resented the fact that high school teachers "blamed" my colleagues, but there were a number of elementary colleagues who were blaming first-grade or kindergarten teachers or parents. When I arrived on the college scene, a number of university professors were blaming both elementary and high school teachers. Eventually it dawned on me that the members of my profession were truly segregated from one another, often placing blame but rarely sharing expertise.

Meanwhile I began to realize that certain teaching-learning strategies encouraged the risk taking necessary for learning. These strategies reflected knowledge about how individuals learn and appeared to work in my various teaching contexts across grade levels and content areas. For example, it seemed to me that first graders need to use their "world views" as a beginning point for school tasks just as fifth graders, eighth graders, twelfth graders, and college students did. Eventually this belief led me to attempt to synthesize current language and learning principles and their practices into a model that could be used by teachers in various grade levels and content areas.

I adopted the varied audience approach in hopes of promoting an exchange among educators of various levels that will lead to sharing expertise and more support and understanding of our colleagues. The ultimate objective is a view of classrooms as communities of learners.

Anna, an elementary teacher who uses CAL in her classroom and has experienced it as an adult learner says,

> Since I've actually experienced it [CAL] at the university level . . . I wholeheartedly believe that it is a process that is applicable to all grade levels and for language arts and content areas. It gives the learner more responsibility and ownership for his or her learning. It actually makes the educational setting a challenging, nurturing and positive environment.

WHY FOCUS ON LANGUAGE AND THINKING IN CONTENT-AREA CLASSES?

There are two reasons to focus on developing language and thinking in content-area classes: (1) to invite all educators to collaborate in promoting students' language and thinking skills; and (2) to provide students with frequent and regular opportunities to use language as a tool for learning.

I am also following the lead of several important educational movements that have developed during the last fifteen years. The whole language movement (led in recent years by Ken and Yetta Goodman) reflects the works of numerous scholar-teachers who have proposed changing the elementary language arts and reading curriculum. Instead of isolated and fragmented drill-and-practice lessons, whole language instruction involves integrating reading, writing, talking, and listening for real purposes, not just in the language arts block but across the curriculum.

Writing across the curriculum movements have emerged at both the secondary and the college level. The National Writing Project, under the direction of Jim Gray, is responsible for providing national leadership to staff development programs for teachers who want to facilitate student writing. One major group of participants in these writing projects consists of content-area teachers from across the curriculum. Colleges and universities have also involved faculty from all disciplines in staff development programs concerned with using writing as a tool for learning. The Faculty Writing Intensive Instruction Seminars, under the direction of Joy Marsella at the University of Hawaii, is one prime example.

While these programs focus on the use of writing as a tool for learning across the disciplines, they also involve lots of talk in small groups, listening, and reading. In other words, they tend to use language as a tool for learning within collaborative activities.

DIFFERENCE IN DEGREE RATHER THAN KIND

What would be the difference between developing language and thinking in reading and writing instruction classes and developing them in content-area classes? The language and learning processes remain the same; the teaching-learning processes remain the same. As I see it, the difference is in the degree of initial guidance novices need to enter the particular domain or content-area.

A primary purpose of reading and writing instruction from elementary school through university is to help students acquire a repertoire of strategies that they can use to construct meaning. In sixth-grade reading, for example, I used to tape a short story, including miscues (such as substituting *home* for *house*); give my students a copy of the short story; and ask them to listen to the tape and mark my miscues. (Students love marking teachers' miscues.) Then I asked them to discuss which miscues changed the meaning of the story. During the discussion, they discovered that miscues weren't such a big deal and that monitoring the text for meaning was what was important, as well as knowing when to correct miscues that changed the meaning. That demonstration was a scaffolding activity in which I tried to guide the students to a better understanding of the reading process and the role of miscues. My goal was to increase their repertoire of strategies to use when reading silently, in this case demonstrating that they didn't have to laboriously "sound out" each word. They could make substitutions, even omissions, as long as they were monitoring for meaning and could self-correct when they went "off the track."

These demonstrations were few and far between; the majority of the time these students were involved in reading silently self-selected materials from any area. The content of the materials reflected a diverse group of students' diverse interests.

In content-area classes, such as English, history, and biology, students also need to have a repertoire of procedural strategies for making sense of the materials. Knowing how to be a member of a problem-solving group, how to respond to peers' writing drafts, and how to look for confirmation of your ideas in the texts are all useful strategies. However, students are also faced with using these strategies to make sense out of particular bodies of knowledge. For novices, the conceptual overload may be too much to handle without some assistance. Thus novices in content-area courses may need more scaffolding activities initially because the activities would help develop both procedural and content knowledge.

The major benefit of an across-the-curriculum focus is that students can develop their language and thinking strategies throughout the school day by being involved regularly in a variety of problem-solving activities that have some meaning to them. To increase the chances that school-related activities have some meaning for students, it is important to give the students access to strategies that allow them to seek answers to their own questions in the particular content area.

HOW TO INCLUDE STUDENT INTERESTS

I believe that the CAL model makes room for student intentions by sharing control. The model suggests a teaching-learning process that starts with what the students already know and what they want to know about the content area and uses student-generated information as the basis for developing or modifying class concepts. The teacher's and students' goals share the class agenda.

The recognition that students enter the class with diverse background knowledge lends itself to an acceptance of varying student opinions. In the collaborative small groups, for example, students look for consensus on an issue, but not at the expense of conformist thinking. Students also use both the small groups and the expressive writing activities, such as think/write logs and focused freewritings, to modify the course direction, to ask for personal assistance, and to initiate questions. Long-term projects, such as investigative (I-Search) papers and field experiences, involve self-selected topics and choice of teaching sites.

I have included a couple of student excerpts to illustrate student reaction to having some choice. A college student has this to say about choosing her own research topic:

> I like the idea of my research topic choosing me, instead of my 'hemming and hawing' over an idea that I'm expected to explore rather than one that means something to me.

Excerpts from elementary students' logs show agreement:

> What I liked about the lesson was about the choices. I didn't not like anything.

> I liked the project because we got to do whatever we wanted to do reserch on. It was hard but I got threw with it. Well I think that was fun

This elementary teacher believes these self-selected projects worked so well because:

> The children wanted to know more about what they could choose (for a topic). They seemed to be motivated and they mentioned in their Think/Write logs that they appreciated the fact they could choose . . . The children themselves asked if they could work together and help each other gather material and share resource material. They learned not only about subject matter but how to work together cooperatively. Problems concerning sharing the material and contributing came up, but they seemed to manage alright . . . Allowing the children to choose (or at least some options) seemed to be the key to their success. They decided on a topic that was meaningful to themselves and that was it. It was easy for them to gather information and focus their reading as they choose the information that was meaningful to them. Because it has a lot of relevance to them, they wanted to share . . . .

Logs also help students indicate to the teacher when their intentions are not being met. I find that it takes students a while to trust the collaborative nature of the teacher-student relationship enough to risk initiating suggestions for change. They have to sense that they will not be penalized for their honesty. For example, in the next log, an undergraduate elementary education major makes clear his displeasure with the way I scheduled the I-Search paper into the semester, and he makes suggestions for modification of this task for my future classes:

> Dr. Bayer, I tossed this back and forth for awhile before I finally decided to share it. On the whole, I enjoyed working on my "I" Search paper. The more I pursued my subject, the more I wanted to learn about "language across the curriculum" . . . I couldn't though, time would not permit. It hasn't been that I've been able to work on a research paper during my studies at the college . . . Sure I've worked on unit plans, lesson plans, evaluations, but rarely on a research paper. If I could recommend, assign the paper earlier. This would entail some reorganizing as far as your syllabus goes. Maybe it could be introduced at the end of the first semester.

The premise of this model is to provide learners with meaningful school-related activities. I believe it is important that students feel comfortable enough to negotiate with the instructor for modifications of strategies and assignments so that the activities in which they are engaged make sense to them. During my twenty years as a teacher-learner I have come to trust that given the opportunity and practice my students provide the most insightful suggestions for improving my courses.

WHAT ABOUT
MULTICULTURAL CLASSROOMS?

All my classes are multicultural, as are the majority of classrooms of the other teachers who will describe their use of the CAL model in later chapters. This collaborative-apprenticeship process is broad enough to be appropriate in multicultural contexts. For example, all responses to the focused freewriting and brainstorming activities are valid. An underlying premise for the model is that students approach topic x differently due to their different experiences, including diverse cultural experiences. The strategies used to build on this student knowledge provide learners with several modes for undertaking a school-related task. Students have room to maneuver and find a culturally compatible niche. For example, they can choose to engage in learning activities by talking in front of the whole class, talking primarily to peers in small groups, writing privately to the instructor in a log, and working independently or primarily in collaboration with others.

Beverly, a history teacher in a multicultural classroom, has this to say about using the model:

> I feel the CAL framework would only help the learning of students from different cultures. Allowing students to write what they know would help the teacher decide where to begin when introducing a new concept . . . Students of different cultures may not feel secure or confident responding to the teacher during class period . . . if students are allowed to talk (with each other) about what they know, they can comfortably share different viewpoints without feeling embarrassed about it. Engaging all the students in scaffolding activities can help them learn from each other. Their cultural differences may then offer another perspective of things and become complementary. Unwilling and fearful to ask questions, the teacher can use the think/write logs to respond individually to these students.

But what does the CAL teaching model look like in a classroom? How would a teacher begin? These questions are addressed in the following chapter.

PART TWO

CASE STUDIES

This part illustrates what a classroom might look like when the teacher and students are engaged in collaborative-apprenticeship learning (CAL). Included are the teaching strategies used to "get started" in a specific class, as well as a description of how the class changed as students increasingly assumed more responsibility for their own learning.

Excerpts from the work of K–12 content-area teachers appear throughout this section to show how you can adapt the CAL model to fill various teaching situations while remaining true to the model and its underlying principles.

3

GETTING STARTED

CASE STUDY CLASS

It may be difficult to get a sense from the CAL charts of how collaborative-apprenticeship learning changes during the school year as students gradually increase their responsibility for their own learning and become more independent. Therefore, in these next two chapters I've decided to use a detailed description of one of my courses to illustrate how I used CAL to get my class started and how the class changed as my students assumed more responsibility.

The course, entitled "Reading and Writing in the Content Area," is offered to both undergraduate students and experienced teachers returning to school. The class meets for a three-hour session once a week for fifteen weeks. It is modeled on the CAL framework so students can have first-hand experience with how it feels to be a learner in this particular teaching-learning process.

K–12 teachers contribute to these two chapters by providing examples of strategies they used to implement the same processes in their classrooms. There are longer K–12 descriptions in Part III.

ELICITING PRIOR KNOWLEDGE

At the first session I begin by asking my students to write down their personal interests and the specific questions they want addressed during the course of the semester. This information guides my planning, and I encourage students to monitor how well their interests are incorporated into class activities. This is my attempt to create a shared agenda from day one.

Then I move (1) to make the students conscious of what they currently believe about using language to promote learning; (2) to examine these beliefs to determine their origins; and (3) to ask what they will do if during the semester they come face to face with evidence that conflicts with what they believe. This approach begins with the students' prior knowledge, and it demonstrates that a teacher's belief system influences what a teacher values in the classroom. Because this is true, it is a professional responsibility for teachers to be conscious of their own belief systems.

Their view of how language can be used to promote learning reflects the students' past experiences, including (1) their personal experiences as a K–12 student; (2) their "book" knowledge about language and learning development; (3) their teaching experiences; and (4) the values of the community in which they live.

To begin the process of raising their beliefs to a conscious level, I ask the students to write for five minutes on the question, "How can language be used to promote learning in the content areas?" The directions I give to the students indicate that I am not going to evaluate this writing for form:

> There is no one correct answer. Don't worry about style or form. Just keep writing for the five minutes.

When the first minutes are up, I explain that the type of writing task they have just completed is called focused freewriting and is one way to use writing as a tool for learning. In this case, I explain, I was using it to elicit their knowledge on a given topic. As the students share their freewritings, first in small groups and then with the whole class, we gain a sense of the class members' current beliefs about using language as a tool for learning. Making these beliefs public gives both the instructor and class members access to at least some of the class's knowledge about this subject. Excerpts from that freewrite discussion follow:

> How can language be used to promote learning in the content areas?
> Language leads to reading, writing. The content areas involve reading (decoding, comprehension) and unless students acquire this skill, (they) can't read, can't comprehend, can't do subject matter. The content areas are just as important as reading, writing because it *uses* reading and writing. Purpose for learning to read and write is to do science, health, social studies, etc. Need content area for broad growth and prep for living in real world (outside of parents' homes and under parents' supervision). Language is the service for learning. Without this acquirement, very difficult to do other things . . . Language can be used to promote learning by doing.

The students use expressive language for these focused freewrites and discussion activities.

Reading	Writing	Talking/Listening
1. Describe the reading assignments in your content areas, K–12.	1. Describe the writing assignments in your content areas, K–12.	1. Describe the talk/ listen assignments in your content areas, K–12.
2. Which activities do you remember as positive? Why?	2. Which activities do you remember as positive? Why?	2. Which activities do you remember as positive? Why?
3. Which activities do you remember as negative? Why?	3. Which activities do you remember as negative? Why?	3. Which activities do you remember as negative? Why?

Next I ask them to examine their personal experiences as K–12 students because these experiences play a role in their current belief systems. The task is to write responses in one of the three categories shown above. I ask students to come prepared to share their responses at the next session.

As soon as the next class begins, I divide the class into small groups of three students responding to the same category. They share their personal experiences of how language was used in content-area classes when they were K–12 students.

The directions for these short-term problem-solving groups are quite similar throughout the semester. Typically I ask the students to take turns reading aloud their focused freewrites. The other group members are to listen for similarities and differences between what is being read and what they themselves wrote. After everyone is finished sharing, they are to compile the similarities and differences on paper. For this task they select the most typical positive memories and the most typical negative memories to share with the whole class. Specific directions like these give novice learners a way to begin to look for connections between other people's ideas and their own. This part of the activity takes about fifteen minutes.

This is the first of many small group sessions that the students will engage in throughout the semester. It is an example of using expressive talk as a tool for learning within a collaborative setting. The group members begin with their own experiences or interpretations of a task and use each other as resources to clarify and expand their thinking. Because this task asks only that the individual recall personal experience, there is no need for preteaching before the group work. Three seems to be a good number for problem-solving groups because it is difficult to "withdraw" from such a small group process without being noticed, which makes it possible to deal with why a group member is not participating.

MEMORIES

How Was Language Used in Your Content Classes, K–12?

Activities That Left Negative Memories	Activities That Left Positive Memories
Questions at end of text	Preteaching
Lectures	Student control: chooses own problem and topic
No preteaching	Learn through concrete activities
Mechanical (responses to writing)	Students allowed to share interests
Focus on form, not comprehension	Interaction (with other students)
Assigned topics	Role playing
Only audience is teacher (for evaluation)	Interviewing
No student control	Guest speakers
Student opinions not allowed	Story telling
Book reports—no involvement	

At the end of the small group discussions, each group writes its findings on the board, listing typical positive and negative memories. The sample shown above is from last spring semester's class.

At this point we examine these memories as a whole class. Students conclude that the "negative memories" activities left them feeling frustrated and unsuccessful as learners because they had no control over the task and because they had difficulty making sense of the task. I take this student-generated content and place it within the categorical scheme "form follows function." Labeling the negative memories as activities that appear to be divorced from a functional or meaningful purpose for the students, I make the argument that appropriate language forms develop as students use language for functional (real) reasons.

This process—starting with what the students know about a given concept, making that information public, engaging students in an activity to expand on what they know, and placing student-generated information within a categorical scheme reflecting the topic under discussion—is the scaffolding structure outlined in the model. I use this structure several times during the early part of the semester. As the apprentice learners begin to assimilate the major concepts, they take over more responsibility for their learning, and the structure is no longer needed.

In the following box K–12 teachers share strategies they use to elicit student knowledge and build on it. While these teachers remain true to the collaborative-apprenticeship learning model, they use various teaching strategies to meet the needs of their particular teaching context. Anna, for example, uses webbing instead of freewriting to elicit student knowledge.

K–12 TEACHERS APPLY
CAL PRINCIPLES

ELEMENTARY

Anna, a first-grade teacher, integrates reading and writing instruction with her science curriculum. The following excerpt is taken from her unit on the ocean. Because they live in Hawaii, the ocean plays a major role in her students' lives. Anna begins this unit from the students' frame of reference by eliciting their knowledge about the ocean. Instead of using a focused freewriting activity, Anna begins with webbing. In her own words:

> Yes, indeed, I always look forward to my Mondays, because Mondays are when I find out how much my students know about a new subject matter. I usually start out with a webbing chart (see below), or a "word explosion" as the children like to call it, to elicit prior knowledge. This oral discussion triggers many ideas and experiences which the children try to connect to the topic.

Procedures for webbing vary, but typically the instructor or a student places the major topic under discussion in a circle on the board, and the students call out whatever comes to mind about the subject. The individual student's contribution is recorded on the board, and either the teacher or another student begins to connect the student-generated information into categories. Anna and her students' webbing chart on the ocean looked like the chart on page 36.

Anna then takes both the collective knowledge, which is now public, and individual student interests into consideration when she makes plans for building on prior knowledge:

> Planning then becomes tailored to where the children are. The children begin to ask questions about what they are curious about, such as, "What's the biggest whale in the world? Can you eat a shark? Do hammerhead sharks eat people?" I explain that books and filmstrips, available from the library, will help us learn about these things. Through the course of the unit, more items are added to the webbing chart and information is written down to answer their questions.

Anna's scaffolding activities are very concrete, often spinning off into

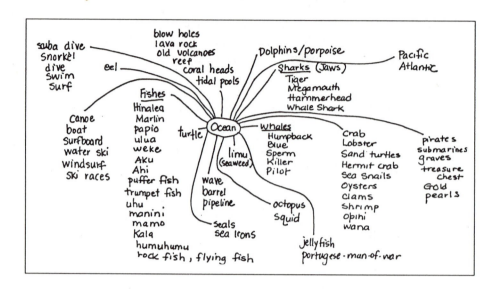

longer-term projects. Reading, writing, and talking play important roles throughout this process:

> We take a field trip to the Waikiki Aquarium. [We] cut out, paint and make stuffed fish. PUPPETS ON THE PATH [an acting company for children] presents an ocean science show educating children on the principles of environmental conservation and protection. Multiple copies of books on this content area are used for reading. We do sponge printing using ocean animals to do subtraction and addition problems. The children also become engaged in writing projects and writing in learning logs about whales, sharks, fish, dolphins, and the ocean.

SECONDARY

On the secondary level, Beverly, a seventh- and eighth-grade social studies teacher, also begins the introduction of new ideas by using the students' frames of reference. In her American history class, she elicits student knowledge about the Declaration of Independence through a focused freewrite question. The following are examples of the responses exactly as they were written:

Student #1

To me, the Declaration of Independence reminds me about the U.S. and England. How we wanted to be independent so much and now we have it. It reminds me of me and my mom arguing about me standing alone without needing her help. It makes me wonder how we came to be a mother and child country and if England is our mother country why do we sometimes call it a foreign place? I think the Declaration of Independence declares us, the child country, to have our independence. I have heard a lot about it but really don't understand it—the true meaning of it.

Student #2

Freedom relates to independence. Independence is when I think my parents let go of me and let me run my life by myself. To take consequences and successes of life. But also to support myself is the main objective of independence. That's what the Declaration of Independence is actually based on—to be free of something—to do the things you want to do, but to work hard, long, and go through some suffering if you are really determined to have it. To go out into the real world when mom and dad aren't there to help you.

The ideas from the students' individual freewrites were shared publicly so all class participants, including the teacher, would have some sense of the collective background knowledge brought to this subject. Picking up on the connections students were making between their own struggle for growing independence and the struggle that took place between the colonies and England, Beverly uses those connections to build on her students knowledge. Her scaffolding activities include student-generated declarations of independence as the precursor for an analysis of the U.S. Declaration of Independence:

Using the blackboard, I illustrated a document which I titled "My Declaration of Independence as a Young Adult." I divided the document into five parts and topics [similar to the U.S. Declaration] and explained the purpose for each section. After doing a sample with the class, the students wrote their own.

Beverly then has her students look for similarities between their declarations and the U.S. Declaration of Independence. She feels they can understand the document and place its meaning in some broader historical perspective because she starts from their frame of reference.

Whether you are a novice teacher who is contemplating student teaching or an experienced teacher returning to the classroom, how would you elicit student knowledge about a particular concept? What strategies would you use to build on that knowledge? Would you provide opportunities for students to collaborate with each other during this process? Would they be able to use expressive language? How would you make room for their interests as well as your agenda?

These scaffolding activities provide not only a vehicle by which apprentice learners can enter a task but also shared knowledge from class participants that can be used as a common reference point to help students assimilate related concepts. In other words the class participants use their shared knowledge as an anchor while negotiating the meaning of new knowledge. For example, I refer to the "memories" activity throughout the semester to help students make connections to related ideas.

After the scaffolding activity in this second session is completed, I raise the question whether (and if so, why) my students are duplicating the negative activities in their own classrooms today. I suggest that as educators we ought to consider modifying some of our teaching practices to reflect new knowledge about language and learning.

For many of these students their K–12 experiences form their schema for how to use language in content areas; this schema is often reinforced by experiences in teacher education institutions and by pressure to have their students do well on standardized tests that assess knowledge of language forms. So it's no surprise that these students, while acknowledging that such traditional instruction may not have worked for them, nonetheless feel ambivalent about questioning its validity.

I periodically raise the question of examining teaching practices to see if our current practices remain valid in light of new knowledge. I use an analogy to other professions to make my point:

> What if your current beliefs are in conflict with the new knowledge? Would you modify your beliefs? Let me ask you a question. Would you return to a doctor who has not modified his practices over the last several decades to reflect new medical knowledge? Has that typically happened in our profession? Do we periodically examine our instruction to see which strategies remain valid given new knowledge and which strategies are invalid and need to be eliminated? Isn't this our responsibility as professionals?

SCAFFOLDING CONTINUES

Raising the issue of "new knowledge" about language and learning development leads the class to an introduction of the concept of how individuals learn.

To introduce this concept, I use a focused freewrite to elicit my students' background knowledge on the subject:

> What is this new knowledge that I'm talking about?
> Let's begin with your current associations.
> Please write for five minutes nonstop. What comes to mind when you read this question, "How do individuals learn?"

Since the purpose of this type of writing assignment is to elicit the students' knowledge quickly, the freewrite is not evaluated or graded.

After the focused freewrite, the students share their responses first in small groups of three and then the small groups share with the whole class. Since the class is heterogeneous, their knowledge of this concept varies, but individuals typically have "bits and pieces" of learning theory. For example, one student wrote

> Individuals usually learn when they can relate it to something they are already familiar with. There are various ways students can learn from textbooks, instruction and even by accident or self-taught. Learning best takes place when the learner is given a model of the concept that is being meant.

Rather than giving a lecture on learning theory I begin with an activity that illustrates individual cognitive processes. This teaching strategy reflects the theoretical perspective that if students have insufficient knowledge on a given topic, the instructor guides the apprentice learners by engaging them in the scaffolding structure process.

I tell the students that I would like to involve them in a task during which they are to look for confirmation of, or conflicts with, the ideas that they generated during the freewrite about how individuals learn. The activity involves problem-solving. I pass around several unidentified tools, such as a red-handled tool used to fix a stuck garbage disposal or a tool for changing an oil filter. Any tools will do as long as they are likely to be unfamiliar to most of the students. I ask the students to examine one tool individually and guess what it is:

> I want to give you a problem to solve. The problem is to figure out what these objects are that I'm going to be passing around the room. Examine one object for a few seconds; jot down everything that comes to your mind as you try to figure out what the object is, and then make a guess.

Students naturally begin to collaborate with each other as they try to figure out what the tool might be, but I remind them that the purpose of this demonstration is to find out what is going on in the mind of each individual. The point that I want to make is that individual learners actively try to construct meaning by using what they already know.

When everyone has had a chance to examine one tool, volunteers begin to share. The students tell me what their guesses are and how they arrived at them. I write all the responses on the board. The following are typical guesses for the garbage disposal tool, known only at this point as the "red thing":

Student #1 Guess: tool to turn on lawn sprinkler
            Why? Gardeners use a similar shape tool to turn on the sprin-
            klers in front of city hall.
Student #2 Guess: tool to pull down patio shades
            Why? Neighbor uses a tool that looks like that to pull down his
            awnings.

Student #3 Guess: a pulley of some kind
     Why? Looks like what is at the end of my clothesline.

Almost always there are a variety of guesses for the same tool. Using this student-generated content, I lead a discussion by raising questions about the guesses:

Why is it that in this group of intelligent individuals we have three different but reasonable guesses for each of the objects? How did each of you make a guess? Right, you each used your past experiences to try to make sense out of this unknown; this object seems to have a function or shape similar to objects you have seen or used before and that led you to make your guess.
     Why are your guesses different? Your prior experiences are different. What implications might this have for your classrooms? Is it reasonable to expect one interpretation of a text when your thirty students also have different past experiences?

My role is to place the student-generated content within a categorical scheme that illustrates several principles of learning, extrapolating the principles from the demonstration:

So let's outline on the board what you have just demonstrated:
You use what you know (past experiences/prior knowledge) to make a guess (prediction, hypothesis). How do you find out if your guess, or we could use the terms *prediction* or *hypothesis*, is correct? Right, you could try out the object to see if it worked. You could ask someone who knows. Let me tell you whose guesses can be confirmed.

After giving the names for all the tools, I fill in the gaps of the theory using technical terms for the first time. *Guess* now becomes *prediction* or *hypothesis*:

If your guess is confirmed you could say that your past experiences served you well; what if your guess was not confirmed? Let's take a closer look at past experiences. Where do they come from? Initially from social experiences that we have as we go about trying to construct meaning in an interactive social context. It would overload our memory, however, if we kept each individual experience separate. So one theory is that we file our representations of individual experiences into different categories or schemata. These schemata become the basis for generating hypotheses about new situations. If the hypothesis (guess, prediction) is confirmed it is assimilated into our existing schemata; if the hypothesis is rejected, we need to modify our existing schemata to accommodate the new information.

Because these ideas are so new to many of my students, I often follow the engagement activity with a concrete example taken from my personal experience of growing up in Maine. There I saw apples growing on trees and using that prior knowledge I guessed that in Hawaii I would see pineapples growing on trees also. Of course, my students, long-term residents of Hawaii, think that's funny. The example does make the point that our past experiences influence our perceptions. Besides demonstrations and concrete examples dramatic activities, videos, field trips, guest speakers, analogies to everyday experiences, and teacher modeling also help students expand their prior knowledge about a new concept.

Excerpts from two of the students' written responses attest to the usefulness of moving from the concrete to the abstract even with college students, when they have insufficient prior knowledge of a given concept:

1. It's clear that concrete experiences are the basis for learning, as well as the entire *interactive social context* of the way we learn something new. I understand that the demonstration on "What is it?" is a good example of the way we learn something new. Also because [the unusual tool] was interesting to us, it caught everyone's attention and helped activate our . . . ideas.

2. I understand how a learner begins with concrete experiences, and uses these experiences to generate a hypothesis. Your example of pineapples growing on trees helped me a lot. It made it easier for me to visualize the concept and process.

FOCUSED READING

Only at this point do I introduce reading assignments. Readers need sufficient background knowledge about a subject to comprehend texts on the subject.

Within the CAL framework, students discover what they already know about a topic, and they build on this knowledge by engaging in scaffolding activities. This preparation increases the chance that students will be able to understand the related text material.

To provide students with a focus for their reading, I usually ask them to look for confirmation of the ideas they generated during their individual freewrites and the scaffolding activity. They are to note which ideas were confirmed and which were not and to come to class prepared to discuss the areas of conflict.

A second strategy you can use to focus student reading is the Informal Prediction Guide (Nicholas 1983). Based on the title of each article students develop two to four questions that they predict will be answered in the article. This is popular with students because they generate their own questions.

Just a note on the reading material I use in my classes. After thinking through the major direction for a course, I search for reading material that can be used to support major course concepts, typically ending up with a couple of books and dozens of journal articles. Students supplement these readings with readings of their own choosing that will best answer their individual questions. My point is that the text material does not dictate the direction of my curriculum.

In the following box K–12 teachers tell how they prepare their students for reading assignments. Here again the teachers choose various teaching strategies to accomplish the same goal of helping their students make connections between prior knowledge and text material.

K–12 TEACHERS APPLY
CAL PRINCIPLES

ELEMENTARY

Linda teaches fifth-grade social studies. Part of the curriculum is concerned with early European explorers:

> I started off with a focused freewrite asking the students to tell me what they think an explorer is and to name some of their favorite explorers. I did this to elicit their prior knowledge ... about explorers. I then broke the students up into groups of four to collaborate by pooling their knowledge. The students used expressive talk and looked for confirmation of their ideas. I had one student record the information so that it would be presented to the class. I used scaffolding activities . . . We then scanned the chapters in the book, discussing the pictures, maps, and bold print, in order to clarify our prior knowledge and make predictions about additional material ... Then I had the students read the text to confirm their predictions.

SECONDARY

Beverly, a seventh- and eighth-grade social studies teacher, also asks her students to make use of their prior knowledge and recent scaffolding activities to make predictions about text material. She asks her students to underline correct predictions as preparation for class discussions on material.

Kathleen, a high school English teacher, developed her own strategy for focusing student reading through a more extensive use of expressive writing. She explains its purpose and how to use it:

> The activity is wonderful for ... preparing students to read a new chapter. It raises questions that the unit or reading may answer ...

STEP 1. Directions for the students.

> Spend the next twenty minutes freewriting (start writing and keep writing) about _____ . Write everything you know, anything you think might be correct, and all the questions you may have.

STEP 2. Directions for the instructor.

> On the board, the overhead projector, or on large sheets of newsprint, make a list of FACTS and QUESTIONS generated (two different pages). Leave these up and refer to them as facts are validated or as questions are addressed (in the text materials).

How would you connect scaffolding activities to reading material? What strategies would you use that are not mentioned here?

HOW MUCH TIME?

The following chart outlines the time spent on the scaffolding and reading activities. These activities elicit what the students know about language and learning and begin to build on this knowledge. Please remember that this is a once-a-week, three-hour block for twenty-five adult students. The CAL process of starting where the students are and beginning to build on it could take up to a week for concept if you had fifty-minute class periods. It is up to you how you implement the process. One of the exciting directions that our profession is taking is to acknowledge that the classroom teacher must take responsibility for making (in collaboration, of course, with peers and administrators) such curriculum decisions as which major concepts within a particular discipline to emphasize and how to do so.

Session 2: 180 Minutes

CAL: Scaffolding Activities	Minutes
1. Sharing freewrites in small groups	10–15
2. Time-out for reflection	15
3. Sharing small group info on board ("memories"); instructor placing info within categorical scheme	45
4. Instructor connecting "memories" with upcoming concept	10
5. Focused freewriting: "How do individuals learn?"	10
6. Sharing in small groups	15
7. Sharing orally with whole class (instructor repeat step 3)	15
8. Students looking for confirmation of their ideas in "tool" demonstration	45
9. Directions for reading material	10

PEERS COLLABORATE
TO CLARIFY

After a short review of what was discussed in the Session 2 the students break up into small groups of three to discuss the readings. In the early part of the semester I usually "count off" groups of three; later in the semester, groups form themselves. My college students told me that at the beginning of a semester not everyone knows everyone. Since individuals may feel left out if not chosen for a group, it's more comfortable if the instructor forms the groups until the class members have a chance to meet each other.

Students are often more helpful than the instructor in explaining concepts to each other (Bayer 1986). They seem to be able to keep their peers' frame of reference in mind. In these small group discussions the students collaborate by expanding and clarifying each others' thinking. I direct the class members to "Share statements from the prediction guide that were not confirmed. See if your group members can help resolve areas of confusion. I will respond to remaining questions."

The instructor's role during these small-group problem-solving tasks is that of a resource person. After fifteen to twenty minutes each group orally shares with the class the ideas from the readings (or demonstration) that are clear, and group members raise any questions they still have. Members of other groups are encouraged to respond to try to give answers; finally I respond to fill in the gaps.

EXPANDING THE ROLE OF
EXPRESSIVE WRITING

Now that we have concretely demonstrated, read about, and discussed the major concept that learners need to make connections between new ideas and prior knowledge, the stage is set for shifting the topic to "How can language assist this process?" I begin by examining the role of writing as a tool for learning.

Again I use focused freewriting to elicit student prior knowledge:

In preparation for next Tuesday's class, take the next five minutes to freewrite on this question, "How can we use writing to help learners make connections between new ideas and their prior knowledge?"

At the beginning of Tuesday's class, I ask the students to engage in a second type of expressive writing, a "think/write" log:

I would like you, in the next ten to fifteen minutes, to write your responses to these questions about how individuals learn:

What is clear?

What is confusing?

What do you want to know more about?

The log allows students to use writing to make tentative connections between the new ideas recently discussed in class and their prior knowledge. It also helps them determine areas of confusion and initiate questions or make statements about their personal interests.

When the students have completed this activity, I label this use of writing as a tool for learning a "think/write" task, tying it to the emerging language and learning principles:

> We need to make connections between our prior knowledge and new ideas to assimilate new ideas. Writing can help learners make sense of new ideas. What kind of writing? In particular, expressive writing.

I introduce and discuss the Britton model of writing (Britton et al. 1975). The major point is that expressive writing is useful when individuals are trying out connections between new ideas and prior knowledge; it is writing used as a tool for learning. Expressive writing has the following characteristics:

- It is the form nearest to speech.
- It is the matrix from which all other writing comes.
- It is crucial for trying out and coming to terms with new ideas.
- It is loosely structured and context bound.
- It makes an assumption of an interest in the writer as a person as well as in his or her subject matter.

Britton's position is that expressive writing is the base for the development of transactional and poetic writing. I think this is particularly true if the topic being written about represents new information for the learner.

Except for their recent experiences with freewriting activities, most of my college students have had little or no experience with using writing as a tool for learning. The idea of a "think/write" log is new to them. As with most new concepts, learners appear to need some guidance. Concrete examples of logs written by former students are especially helpful. The first semester I taught this course I didn't provide any concrete examples for my students and the resulting confusion came out loud and clear in student written feedback:

> As I read through my first entry in the learning log, I remembered the thoughts that ran through my mind at that time. I can remember a lot of confusion of the learning log. I thought to myself, what will I write, how much do I write, I'm not confused by anything we learned, what's this all about? These thoughts were floating around in my head and it never occurred to me, to write about my confusion. Instead, my first entry looked like this:
>
> *When we did the activity on the "silver thing," many things went through my mind . . . the color, shape, size, weight, texture, and the touch. Next, I wondered*

what it could be used for . . . maybe a hook for fishing, or something to hang an object on. During this process, I was actually learning something new. . .

This first entry seemed to be "safe" writing, writing that is neat, carefully punctuated, grammatically clear, with very surface information. The entry was written in pencil with perfect erasure marks. I felt that I was writing just for the sake of writing. I took in the information, processed it, and organized it on a piece of paper. I wrote the entry as if someone was going to read it and give me a grade. And as I ended, I was still confused as to what the learning log was all about or why I had to do it. I summarized a portion of the lecture and tucked the entry away . . . I felt that writing wasn't helping me. I think at this point a model of a learning log would have helped me get started.

In an attempt to eliminate student confusion about think/write logs, and to be theoretically consistent (using concrete strategies to expand prior knowledge), I use an overhead projector to show samples of logs written by students from grade two through college.

This first excerpt is from a first grader who is using a think/write log in her science curriculum:

We terned more about Pant and seeds. And we also no wha we needs. And it is 6 werds and i'll tell you it is sun, wind, soil, fertilizer and the last one is water. I'll tell you why water is inportent. It's becouce water is the drinck of the seed and then the seeds grow big, big, big then the seeds pops out then that means it's growing And that' how it grows. I Don't have any questinos becous I lisened very, very good. That's why i can right alote. And anser alot.

Learning Log– What is confusing?

4/1

We started find the LCD and it's not hard. I understand it, but when we started do'ng cross products I got all confused. For example–

which is bigger

4×1=4
2×3=6

So which

one has more value $\frac{1}{2}$ or $\frac{3}{4}$?

In the learning log above, a seventh-grade basic math student is trying to make sense of fractions.

In the example below, a tenth-grade literature student is stating what he understands about the just-completed unit on Korean literature.

March 4

1) I understand that traditional and modern literatur is divided by western influence. (freedom and independance)
    I understand that that the history goes back some 4000 years. And throughout its history, Korea has been abused a lot by other countries. (war)
    I understand that a lot of the literature deals with separation or other fatalistic themes.
    I understand that Korean people had a love for nature and peace.
    I understand that it is a writers responsibility to reflect the psychology of his/her people and in Korea's case that psychology is filled with sorrow and separation.

Finally I show the class an excerpt from a college student who is writing about what she understands about the reading process:

Tonight's discussion of the reading task was interesting. I found that my reader also deviated from the text and self corrected when the reading didn't make sense. My reader also experienced anxiety about having to read something aloud. I felt the demonstration was worthwhile because I think most of us have forgotten or don't realize the pressure we put students under when we have them read aloud and correct their miscues immediately. It was demonstrated that even "good" readers make errors in reading aloud but that this doesn't necessarily interfere w/comprehension and that if it does the reader will most likely correct himself. It's important for teachers to realize that one doesn't need to process every single word of text in order to compre-hend a message and w/this information in mind reading "instruction" should focus upon helping the child to make sense of text through any and all means available.

The demonstration on how prior knowledge affects comprehension ties in w/what I was just reading in the Langer text and further clarifies the notion that one's prior experiences/knowledge can and does affect comprehension and interpretation of the author's message. The text talked about some of the problems that can arise when the reader interprets the message in a different way and as I was writing my reading response log it became really clear to me that in our practicum where writing is the focus, again, prior knowledge plays such a vital role in how a student learns and how important it is to not only give new information but have the student make connections between that new knowledge and prior experience.

Having shared the concrete examples, students work in small groups (1) to discuss whether today's think/write log demonstration confirmed or rejected their freewriting idea about how writing can assist learning; (2) to help each other clarify areas of confusion; and (3) to see where they can agree on how writing can be used as a tool for learning. As before I act as a resource during the small group discussions; each group shares its findings; and I try to clarify any remaining areas of confusion. As their knowledge base expands, students assume more responsibility for their learning through increased collaboration with each other in small groups.

I now ask the class members to begin keeping a think/write log for this class:

Begin today keeping a think/write log. At first you will share them with me weekly, so a loose-leaf notebook will probably work best. Write every week. I'll try to provide class time, but you will need to write out of class as well. Keep a record of the following information:

1.   What's clear about the ideas being discussed?

2.   What are you confused about?

3.   What do you want to know more about?

You may eventually decide that you will try to answer your own questions. In that case you will turn in your logs only when you cannot find the answers yourself. In any case a record of questions about issues that interest you will be useful when you think about topics for your I-Search papers that will be due later in the semester. The logs are not evaluated or graded.

It was interesting to me to observe the changes in the students' logs during the semester. Initially, most of the learners wrote to me as an evaluator. Only with practice and consistent feedback on the content of the message rather than its form did students use these logs to reflect what they were really thinking. The following excerpts describe one student's reflective analysis of how she used her log:

My first attempt at writing to learn was a mere "regurgitation" of class materials. I did not attempt to assimilate the new information. Here, I am simply writing for the teacher. I paid special attention to the proper use of grammar and punctuation. I made a conscious effort to make both perfect:

February 12, 1985
Individuals learn through concrete experiences. To be embedded into the student's cognitive memory, the new knowledge should have something in common with the learners' prior knowledge. To be more specific, the teacher may model, then have the students practice this same process. It is important that the students first apply the new knowledge, then practice it.

Gradually, instead of simply transferring class notes into my "Think-Write Logs," I began to assimilate new ideas from class lectures. I attempted to connect these new ideas to my prior knowledge about the particular concept being studies. However, I still was writing to inform the teacher of my progress. Hints of my reactions and feelings regarding the lesson or experience began to emerge.

I became totally frustrated with the concept of writing to learn. I felt as though it was a waste of time. "Why write about what I'm learning when I could be doing something more productive?" Clearly, I was not utilizing these logs in the proper manner. These feelings were recorded among my log entries:

March 1, 1985
Why write??? Am I learning anything through writing? No, I don't think so! This is a waste of time—my precious time! Could be working for my colleagues. Why??? Let's see . . . I could try to assimilate new information by using more concrete examples . . . OK, I'll try to write everything in my own words and keep writing until I understand everything.

Ironically, my highest point of frustration proved to be a true turning point in my use of writing to learn. Here, I wanted to learn. My actual thinking process is readily seen through my choice of punctuation and words, "Why???, let's see . . ." The three question marks show the total confusion I was feeling at the time, and the dots indicate pauses in my thinking. I am posing questions for myself and making an attempt to answer these questions.

Gradually, the "Think-Write Logs" became an essential new tool to assist me in understanding course material. In writing new ideas and using my own words, I am able to clarify concepts which I do not understand. Instead of complete sentences with proper grammar and punctuation, incomplete and ungrammatical sentences, along with person symbols, now characterize my "Think-Write Logs":

March 31, 1985

PREP

Phases 1 Key word/concept

2 Why responses?

3 Students verbalize

Level of student's prior knowledge can be seen this way.

If there are any questions I had which emerged during class and while reading the handouts, I would jot them down, then attempt to answer them on my own:

April 9, 1985

Ideational Anchorage??? What does that mean??? Relates to Schemata. *Linking new knowledge to prior experience. I'm not sure...*

In my first attempt to answer the question I posed for myself, I tried to explain it using my own words. However, I still wasn't clear as to what the term "Ideational Anchorage" meant. I further researched the concept in an effort to clarify the meaning. This is what I finally came up with:

Ideational Anchorage:

New Information

Prior Knowledge

Clearly this student had shifted from writing summaries for the teacher to using writing as a tool for her learning. While the majority of students responded positively to the use of logs for learning, there were exceptions:

Write/Think Log—

Well . . . this is the *last* one. My thoughts on write/think logs—

I find them helpful in the specific and timely feedback I got from them. The logs made me think some things through. It helped me "sound out" complicated matters concerning my practicum. I could look back at this record and see changes occurring in my understanding of using writing as a reading tool. I really enjoyed reading your comments.

BUT . . . (hee hee) Although *this* experience w/logs has been 10x more encouraging and *useful* than my previous experiences, I still don't *like* doing the logs. I do them because it's required. I much rather do focused free writings (yikes!!)

Seriously, I do enjoy the FFW. They were more focus and I didn't have to grope for a topic to write about.

I guess journals have never been something that interested me (even as a child).

I did earn some things from writing these logs, but at times it was painful. (joke)

Before turning to the preparation for next week, I add a section called, "Reflections on language and learning uses in this class." This is appropriate within the context of my class because I am working with educators. The purpose is to help raise to a conscious level just how these learners are using language to facilitate their own learning. It's another attempt to make the point that what works for them as learners is likely to work for their own students. The message I hope to get across is not to divorce how they teach from how they learn. The strategy is to have the students "do it" and then reflect on what they have done. In other words, students actually use language as a tool for learning and then make abstract generalizations about what that experience means for their own classrooms. Reflections will be discussed at the end of each session throughout the rest of the semester.

I use a freewrite to focus student reading for the next session and then ask them to look for confirmation of their focused freewrite ideas when they read the handouts:

> In preparation for next week, when we will expand on this topic of expressive writing, please freewrite for five minutes on the question "How could you guide students to move beyond expressive writing to transactional or poetic?" Look for confirmation of your ideas in this week's readings.

Part of the answer to this question will be found in increased peer collaboration, the subject of the next chapter.

4

SHIFTING THE RESPONSIBILITY

INCREASED COLLABORATION

Students usually begin to assume greater responsibility for their own learning about a third of the way through the semester. This comes about through increased use of small group activities. While students have been participating in collaborative joint activities since the first day, the time and type of peer interaction now increases. I continue to set the structure, but the students increasingly control the topics and methods of carrying out their tasks. For example, I use peer writing response groups to help students experience how peer collaboration can help student writers move beyond expressive writing to transactional writing.

Students are also forming practicum support groups about this time. Since the students are required to "try out" CAL in their respective teaching contexts, they meet with others from similar grade levels and content areas to help each other find solutions to their problems. (See the appendixes for practicum information.)

Excerpts from a recent course syllabus, shown on the opposite page, illustrate the increased use of peer collaboration.

In all peer collaborative activities, I use a structure that includes reviewing with the students an agreed purpose for the small group, providing specific directions that will help members begin the small group process, and sharing of the results of the small group work with the whole class.

In the Applications Box beginning on page 54 K–12 teachers share the various strategies they used to set the stage for successful small group collaboration.

READING AND WRITING
IN CONTENT AREAS, K–12

Division	Session	Topic	Out-of-class requirements	Peer groups
1/3	1	Introduction: examining your beliefs		
	2	Language and learning theory		Short, randomly selected sharing and problem-solving groups
	3	Expressive writing	Keep weekly think/write logs	
	4	Preparation for practicum: CAL model; video: "Flight"		
	5	Beyond expressive writing: Preparation for research paper; video: "Snake Hill"		
2/3	6	"Correcting" grammar, spelling, mechanics; *writing response groups (topics);* Preparation for support groups	Begin practicum Begin "I Search" project	Add to problem-solving groups, peer writing response groups, and support groups
	7	Talk as a tool for learning in small groups; *support groups*		
	8	*Writing response groups (revision);* preparation for reading process		
	9	Reading process and prior knowledge: *support groups*		
	10	Stategies for increasing text comprehension; *support groups*	End practicum (option A)	
3/3	11	*Writing response groups (revision): support groups*		All italicized activities are student led
	12	*Writing response groups (editing)*	End practicum (option B);	
	13	*Authors' sharing*	Last think/ write log due;	
	14	*Practicum panels*	I-Search project due; practicum paper due	
	15	Practicum papers due; summary evaluations		

K-12 TEACHERS APPLY CAL PRINCIPLES

ELEMENTARY

As a fifth-grade social studies teacher, Sharon guided the collaborative small group process initially.

> Ridicule was out, and "hitchhiking/piggybacking" on each other's ideas was accepted. In other words, students were encouraged to listen, share, build upon the ideas of others.

How did Sharon help her students understand what she meant?

> As the teacher, I guided them through the process, listened to what they had to say, and did not offer judgment but acceptance. I first modeled what I sought, using students to help, sat in on group discussions in "round table sharing," and primarily allowed ideas to flow, while making suggestions or asking questions for students to ponder along the way.

Evidence of the benefits of collaboration can be seen in a fifth grader's think/write log. What she had learned in class that day about European explorers was clear because "we discosted it together":

> Brenda—Think write log 10/7
> I learned that the Europen sailors took the three routs to get there goods like spices, jewelry, and clothes. I also learned that vikings sailed from Norway to Iceland and to Greenland. Eric's son from the vikings was going back to Norway when he got blown off chores from a storm and he ended up in North America. Everything was pretty clear to me because we discosted it together.

Elizabeth and Anne, kindergarten teachers who collaborated on a plan to implement CAL in their classroom, added the role of reporter to their small group processes:

> Our final modification [was] using "reporters" to publicize the knowledge [generated] from the group. The reporter gained a sense of importance and increased confidence. She found it necessary to listen carefully to everyone's comments and then to pick one important idea . . . to share with the class.

SECONDARY

In Wayne's high school science classes, members of collaborative small groups are encouraged to "piggyback" on each others' ideas. In a handout, Wayne tells students to:

Discuss your answers. Please share your answers. Jot down any suggestions your neighbor might have. Remember scientists are always coming up with theories, sharing them, then trying to confirm or discard them.

All of the above groups, from kindergarten, fifth grade, and high school were heterogeneous.

How would you prepare your students for increased small group work? What scaffolding activities would you use to guide them as they increase the time and kinds of small group collaboration?

Most of the K–12 teacher comments focused on problem-solving groups used for short periods of time. The next section, will describe preparation for student involvement in long-term groups.

TRANSACTIONAL WRITING PREPARATION

My students' first long-term project is an investigative paper in which they search for answers to their own questions. To prepare for the project the students engage in activities that illustrate both the reasons for transactional writing pieces and the peer processes that can help them produce such pieces.

I review for the students that this course focuses on how learners use language as a tool for learning and that we have been discussing using expressive writing as a tool for learning. So far we have demonstrated two examples of expressive writing: (1) focused freewrites to elicit student knowledge on a new topic and to focus reading; (2) think/write logs to raise to a conscious level connections between a new topic and student prior knowledge and areas of confusion that are interfering with assimilation of new concepts.

In most content areas we teachers want our students to move beyond tentative connections and become able to argue, inform, persuade, or share their interpretations of new knowledge with more public audiences. The question I pose is how teachers can help students move beyond expressive writing to transactional writing. Since the students have already completed a focused freewrite on this topic, they meet in small groups to share their individual knowledge, collaborating to generate a shared group perspective. They also look for confirmation of this perspective as they participate in two demonstrations intended to illustrate (1) how purpose and audience influence language style and genre; and (2) how to guide students toward transactional writing.

The first concrete demonstration used to illustrate the influence of audience and purpose is an adaptation of the paradigm Moffett (1981) illustrates in his "I, YOU and IT" essay. My directions to the students include:

1. Identify a place where you go often (airport lounge, cafeteria, etc.). Imagine yourself in that place. Without worrying about form, record what is happening now around you.
2. Now imagine you are with a friend; relate to him or her what happened. Write your account as if you were telling her of your experience.
3. Now take that same experience and think of it as something that recurs. Write to an unknown audience for publication to explain why such an experience might happen. (If you frequently have observed someone getting angry at the ticket agent, for example, you might conclude that traveling produces anxiety.)

The students spend five to eight minutes on each step, and then volunteers read their pieces aloud. The following is one response taken from last semester's class.

The first excerpt reflects expressive writing, which is "loosely structured and context bound" (Britton et al. 1975). The student is describing the backstage scene at a community college theater after a performance.

> LCC students moving around, ownership, confidence, cocky, show-off, pride, camaraderie, Don—fish-in-water, moving from student, confident, easy

The author's second piece reflects a shift away from expressive writing as the author relates to a friend what happened.

> I was backstage at Lockgreen Community College last night for the Spring Semester offering of faculty and students.
> The show was a fifties hop recreation only the fifties never saw such organization. After the show the faculty who had dominated the solo numbers in the show stood around and assured each other that they had done a fantastic job of showing these students "real theatre."

The language here is more explicit, but it remains informal given the personal audience. In the last excerpt, addressed to an unknown audience for publication, the genre shifts toward exposition.

> There is a constant battle in educational theatre with impassioned advocates on both sides: the "we learn by example," group and the "we learn by experience" group. I have learned under both schools, but my preference is for the experience group.
> Lockgreen Community College has had a drama program for x years. In that time the faculty, staff, and students have produced seven memorable theatre pieces, including Hotel Street and 10'o. They also produced The Fifties Hop, which I saw on Saturday night.
> The students were given very minor crowd scenes to play, while LCC faculty and performers from outside the college sang major roles.
> I feel the students were cheated. If role models were needed to help a student sing "In the Jungle," they should have worked as coaches, not performers.

We reflect as a class on what has been illustrated through the student's examples; that is, when a writer changes audience and purpose, the genre of the writing piece changes. This task is an attempt on my part to demonstrate that (1) form follows function, and (2) expressive writing can be used as a basis for transactional writing. In other words, authors start with expressive writing and reshape or revise their writing to meet the needs of various audiences.

The second demonstration illustrates the process of guiding students from expressive to transactional writing. In an attempt to model at the university what I suggest these teachers do in their K–12 classrooms, I ask my students to engage in this process for their required research papers. They "walk through" the suggested procedures themselves, and then we reflect on what worked and what didn't.

The process is a modified version of Ken Macrorie's I-Search paper (1980, 1984, 1985). For the next class session I ask the students to work their way through the following Step 1 and come prepared to share their topic choice with members of a peer response group. These peer response groups have the same function as writing groups; they allow learners to participate in joint activities as a way of facilitating their learning.

STEP 1: Choosing Your Topic

> Try to let the topic choose you from your think/write log or free writing; from walks; from conversations with friends; from your reading, watching, and doing. Your topic needs to be something that you want intensely to know.

> Make a list of at least five topics you are curious about researching.

> Choose two of these and do a five-minute free writing on each.

> Develop a question from each of your five-minute writings.

> As you write, think about what you already know about this topic and what you want to find out.

STEP 2: The Search

> Once you've got a topic, take it to class or the group you're working with, tell the others how you became interested in it, and ask them if they can help you with tips, names, addresses, phone numbers of experts, and so on.

THE SHIFT

In the next class session, students share their topic choices with the whole class, form groups of five or six based on similar topic interests, and meet with their groups to get suggestions for research sources on their topic. For the rest of the semester, at least half of each session's three-hour block is used by students working with each other in various small groups. During this time the instructor acts as a resource for the group members when needed. Notice that the responsibility for choosing and carrying out problem-solving activities is increasingly shifting to the students.

Directions for this peer response group session are:

1. Each person in the group has a turn.
2. Share your topic choice and how you became interested in that topic.
3. If your topic is broad, ask for help in narrowing it.
4. Ask for suggestions for firsthand and secondhand sources for research.
5. You will have approximately forty-five minutes, so each group member has just under ten minutes.

At the end of forty-five minutes, I remind the students to begin their research during the week and come prepared with a first draft in two weeks. I outline suggestions for conducting the research (again taken from Macrorie) in a handout:

1. Find experts or authorities. Ask them where to locate the most useful books, magazines, newspapers, films, tapes, or experts on your topic.
2. Look at or listen to this information and these ideas. Note what may be useful to you.
3. Before you interview people who know a lot about your topic, think about the best way to approach them. Through another person who knows them? Directly by telephone or letter?
4. Consult both firsthand sources (people who talk to you about what they're doing or your own observations of objects and events) and secondhand sources (books, magazines, newspapers, or people who tell you about what others have done).

Students share their early drafts, which reflect the findings of their research, with peer response groups to receive feedback on the clarity of the message. Editing groups will meet later.

I make a point of separating peer responses to the message from peer responses to language form because my students have typically had experience only with "correcting" language form (or being corrected) as a method of responding to writing pieces. The process of revising for clarity of ideas is not built into most content-area instruction. I argue that focusing on the clarity of the message aids in the development of appropriate language forms I remind them of the "memories" activity and of their own experiences in which form was emphasized exclusively. Roman, a novice high school history teacher, shares his perspective on the place of form in the process of developing language and thinking:

I think it is very important for students to understand that the critical thinking process is a "messy" one; that solid gold wisdom does not come forth without struggles, revisions, dead-ends, and so on. The most successful writers, be they novelists or historians or sociologists, are constantly revising, throwing away, adding onto their opinions, thoughts, and "big ideas." It is not an easy process, but it can be an exciting, or at least a meaningful, experience for those who are willing to put forth the effort ... After the student is actively engaged and struggling and playing with content, then the teacher can focus on form— showing the student that if he believes his insights are worthwhile, he must be able to communicate them effectively to an audience larger than himself. In fact, proper form makes his ideas even clearer to himself.

EXAMINING "TALK"

While half our class time in this middle part of the semester is used for long-term collaborative projects such as the I-Search paper, the other half is used to explore additional concepts related to the overall topic of using language as a tool for learning. So while the students are conducting their I-Searches outside of class, in Session 6 we begin examining the role that "talk" plays in learning. I use an informal prediction guide:

> In preparation for next week's topic, "talk as a tool for learning," please generate two or three questions based on the title of this handout [an article on Vygotsky] that you predict will be answered in the text.
> Read for confirmation of your predictions.

When class reconvenes, I first ask students to share in groups of three the results of using the informal prediction guide:

> In small groups, share your prediction guide questions and use the information in the article to illustrate which of your questions were confirmed.
> Secondly see if you can reach a consensus on the question "What connections, if any, do you see between the CAL framework and Vygotsky's concepts?" The second task will be tape-recorded, so please be sure to test your equipment to see if your voices are being recorded clearly.

Taping the sessions will illustrate concretely the benefits of using small groups in the classrooms. Apprentice educators are often told that small groups are "good," but they don't understand why. By analyzing their own talk they can demonstrate to themselves how talk can be used as a tool for learning. After a fifteen- to twenty-minute discussion period we share the different groups' responses. The majority of the groups connect the collaborative-apprenticeship notion with Vygotsky's zone of proximal development concept (ZPD).

We then move on to the analysis of their own talk. My instructions to the groups are:

Play your group's tape and write down examples of the following:

1. *Someone stating that they are not clear about what to do.* This might be reflected on the tape as "I'm not sure what we're to do."

2. *Someone using their past experiences in the discussion.* An example would be something like, "I tried to think back when I was young . . ."

3. *Someone initiating a point.* The language might be, "I think that . . ." or "I guess that . . ."

4. *Someone adding to what someone else said.* These might be, "Yeah, that's like . . . ," "Yeah, and *another* thing related to that . . . ," or "Right, right, also . . ."

5. *Someone disagreeing with a group member.* These might be, "Yeah, but . . ." or "No, I don't think so." In this case write the responses until the disagreement is resolved.

It might be helpful to have each member of the group listen for one type of example. Take the next fifteen minutes to find as many examples as you can.

At the end of fifteen minutes the class reassembles and each group writes examples from each category on the board. It is fascinating to me that every semester all groups find examples that reflect each of the five categories.

As I read the examples aloud, I reflect on the hypotheses generation, collaboration, and language growth that these examples represent. For example, "I think that talk is better because when I was in second grade we had 'Show and Tell' and . . ." shows a learner who is generating hypotheses based on prior knowledge to make sense of the task. The examples of statements of confusion, adding to what someone else said, disagreement, and responses to these statements all illustrate the Vygotskian perspective that learning is facilitated through collaboration as group members clarify, expand, and make more explicit their own and each other's thinking.

The disagreement statements are particularly good illustrations of students faced with differing viewpoints. While presenting their arguments, students become more logical in their thinking and more explicit in their language. It is the process in which negotiation and co-construction of meaning is most evident.

The student response to this demonstration is favorable:

Our taped discussions of shared connections between the CAL framework and proximal development were an excellent example of scaffolding in working with mixed ability groups. Group members who understood better or knew more scaffolded for those who were unsure, confused, and knew less. Initial intimidation by the presence of the recorder wore off quickly, though it did serve to minimize "overlapping"—members tended to take turns speaking more than usual . . . .

Another student shares her reaction to becoming conscious of the role talk plays in her learning:

I feel a bit embarrassed about turning in my log last week. In it, I rambled on about trusting only journals and professors and not my fellow peers when learning new information. I take it back! Last week when the class formed groups and talked abut Vygotsky's theories on the tape recorder, I trusted myself the least. Then you said later how different people have different strengths and how those people bring a lot to the group. Depending on the topic, a new group member may bring in a lot of background knowledge to help the group move along. I also have been thinking about my own ways of learning new information. Although I said that I felt that I learned only through reading books and journals, I also learn through talking with others about that information. Sometimes it doesn't really feel like "my" knowledge unless I tell it to others or write it down, then tell it to others. Last week I didn't even think about what I did *after* I read or after I heard a lecture. I also realize that learning doesn't only occur in school learning groups, it occurs when you see or hear strangers talking about unfamiliar things you'd like to know more about or when a mechanic decides to teach you a few things about cars. People with experience don't necessarily write books or teach at the university—they come from all walks of life and are the ones we try to learn from.

Again and again the feedback from my students points out the importance of expanding on insufficient prior knowledge through concrete demonstrations and examples regardless of age of learner.

HOW MUCH TIME?

The following chart illustrates how much time my students and I spent on various activities during this last class. Compare this with the chart on page 43 to get an idea how the transfer of responsibility is shifting during the middle part of the course. Note the increase in time spent in small groups.

SESSION 7: 180 MINUTES

CAL: Increasing Peer Collaboration	Minutes
1. Returning logs and review	15
2. Sharing informal prediction guide results in small groups (taped)	20
3. Sharing small group results with whole class; instructor making connections between ideas	20
4. Analyzing own "talk" in same small groups	30
5. Sharing results of analysis on board; instructor placing information within categorical system and connecting to earlier discussion	45
6. Students meeting in practicum support groups	45

THE LAST CONCEPT:
READING

Parts of the next three sessions deal with the last major course topic, the reading process. If you check the syllabus (p. 53), you can see how the examination of reading is spread over these three sessions and divided in the following ways:

Session 8: Preparation for reading process

Session 9: Reading process and prior knowledge

Session 10: Strategies for increasing text comprehension

Once again I return to an earlier part of the CAL model for strategies to help my students make connections between their knowledge about reading and new ideas that may come up in class. We examine the reading process generally first and then within content-area curriculums. I elicit the students' prior knowledge of the reading process through a focused freewrite. Their current beliefs will be either confirmed or rejected as they participate in their first out-of-class assignment on this subject.

> Let's begin with a focused freewrite. Please write for five minutes in response to this question, "How do good readers read?" Look for confirmation of your ideas in the demonstration I'm going to ask you to carry out this week outside of class. Pick a partner, an adult who is a good reader, and have that person read aloud to you something they have not read before for five to ten minutes. Sit beside your partner with a photocopy of the text and write down the answers to these questions:
>
> 1. Did the reader say anything different from what is in the text? Give examples.
> 2. Did the reader always correct these deviations? Give examples.
> 3. Did the reader understand the text? Give your thoughts on why or why not.

In the ninth session, students report on the results of the "good reader" demonstration. The students indicate by a show of hands how many had good readers who deviated from the text. The majority had. Volunteers put examples of deviations on the board. They list what the text is, what the reader said, and whether the reader self-corrected. Donna reports on a fellow university student:

> 1. Things she said differently:
>   a. "Perfect" instead of "perfectly"
>   b. She added "a" in the following phrase: "and *a* drop of soy sauce."
>   c. "Into" instead of "onto"

  d. "You" instead of "who"
  e. "Some carrots" instead of "more carrots"
  f. "Everything" instead of "anything"
  g. Deleted "up" from "raised it *up* to his mouth"
  h. Deleted "have" from "It must *have* come to"

Then we go over the deviations, examining which ones changed the meaning and which ones were corrected. It typically turns out that only the deviations that changed the meaning were corrected. Students often also discover that the friends who read for them were anxious about their reading performance and their comprehension suffered because of it.

In my summary I begin to place the student-generated information within a conceptual framework. I point out that the demonstration shows that good readers do not read each word exactly; they substitute, omit, and add words. Good readers do not correct themselves every time they make a deviation; they usually do so only when they have changed the meaning. Finally, if good readers are focusing on their oral performance, their comprehension of the text material suffers. I remind students to be conscious of whether the predictions they generated from their focused freewrite on "how good readers read" are being confirmed or rejected.

Another demonstration that illustrates the reading process involves my own students' reading strategies. The activity includes two transparencies, each with a paragraph of about the same length. The first paragraph, which follows, is about writing in the elementary classroom, a topic this audience should comprehend with ease:

> In our view, the elementary school curriculum today is turning more attention to writing skills. Children are writing more than they used to, on topics of personal and imaginative interest to them. Teachers have begun to provide a wider array of stimuli for writing experiences and to view them as important to the development of skills in reading, speaking, and listening. Creative writing has become a staple rather than a luxury in the elementary classroom, and that is encouraging.

The second paragraph is an excerpt from a section on probability in a statistics text, a topic this audience will probably have insufficient prior knowledge to comprehend:

> These 8 possibilities are grouped to show that there is 1 possibility giving 0 heads, 3 possibilities giving exactly 1 head, 3 possibilities giving exactly 2 heads, and 1 possibility giving 3 heads. The 3 ways of getting exactly 2 heads arose from two sets of possible outcomes for N=2. Those which contain exactly 1 head and the one containing exactly 2 heads. Thus, the number of possibilities for N=3 containing 2 heads (3) is the number of possibilities for N=2 containing exactly 1 head (2), plus the number of possibilities for N=2 containing exactly 2 heads (1).

I place the first paragraph on the overhead projector and ask the students to read it silently. Then I ask volunteers to paraphrase the content. The majority of students are able to paraphrase this paragraph with little difficulty.

I repeat the process for the second paragraph. This time, however, only one or two students can paraphrase the content. The difference in student response leads to a discussion about the reading process generally. In both cases the students could pronounce all the words; therefore something else must be needed to read for meaning. I ask

> How many can paraphrase this second paragraph? Only two? Could you pronounce all the words? Yes. So if you could pronounce all the words in both paragraphs, why is there a difference in comprehension? Yes, you need prior knowledge about the topic in the text. Are we back to the constructivist theory again? Does prior knowledge play a role in the reading process as well?

I expand the connection between an individual's prior knowledge and reading comprehension by reexamining what happened in the "good reader" demonstration.

> We noted in the first demonstration today that good readers do not read every word but often deviate from the text. What are they doing? They are using prior knowledge to make predictions (generate hypotheses) that help them make sense of the text. Good readers process just enough print to see if their predictions are being confirmed. If we are making meaning we keep reading. If we begin to become confused, our predictions are being rejected and we may have to go back to self-correct.

These two demonstrations lead to a discussion of the sociopsycholinguistic reading model (Goodman & Burke 1972; Goodman 1986; Smith 1985; Harste, Woodward & Burke 1984; Weaver 1988) in preparation for the next session's work on the implications this model has for learning from texts in content areas.

As in the previous weeks the students' spend about fifteen minutes writing in their think/write logs questions they might have about this model of reading. Then I ask them to generate questions for an informal prediction guide they can use to focus their reading; the topic for the prediction guide is "reading in the content areas":

> In preparation for our next session's discussion on reading in the content areas please develop two or three questions based on the titles that you predict will be answered in each of these articles: "Using prediction to increase content area interest and understanding" [Nicholas 1983], and "Prediction Guides: A Subject Area Teachers' Best Friend" [Leonard 1982].
> Look for confirmation of your predictions when you read the articles.

In the session 10 I briefly review the reading process as illustrated in last session and then shift the focus to the the use of the reading process in content areas. To demonstrate how reading is used traditionally in many content area classes, I place the following paragraph on the overhead projector:

An interesting modern example of back formation suffix involves the word *laser*. Recall that this word is an acronym; it ends in *er* only because *e* stands for *e*mission and *r* stands for *r*adiation (*L*ight *A*mplification (by) *S*timulated *E*mission (of) *R*adiation). Recall, though, that speakers quickly forget such origins, and before long physicists had invented the verb *to lase,* used in sentences such as, "This dye, under the appropriate laboratory conditions, will lase." Where *to lase* refers to emitting radiation of a certain sort. The *er* on *laser* accidentally resembles the agentive suffix *er,* and the word itself refers to an instrument. Hence, physicists took this *er* sequence to be the agentive suffix and subtracted it to form a new verb.

How did physicists create a back formation to form a new verb?

I ask the students to read the paragraph silently and then tell me what it means. Few students have sufficient prior knowledge on this subject to comprehend the ideas in the text. Then I ask if they can answer the question without understanding the concept. Many can because they can literally match up enough of the text to make a reasonable guess.

This exercise illustrates how reading is used in many content-area curriculums. The students are asked to read the chapter and answer the questions at the end. Yet, although many of these college students were successful in answering the question they could not really understand the text. As *their* teacher, should I recommend a remedial reading class for them because they can't read a text with comprehension? Should I be satisfied that they can complete an instructional task even when it makes no sense to them?

College students hardly think they need remedial reading instruction. They get quite indignant at the thought. Yet isn't that the option many content-area teachers use when their students don't understand the text? At this point I tie this activity to the language and learning principles developed during the semester.

I hope the students make the connections that (1) this activity of reading the text and answering the questions at the end of it makes no provision for variability in student prior knowledge and (2) no concrete experiences have been introduced to expand prior knowledge before reading. If students have insufficient knowledge of the text topic they cannot make predictions or construct meaning.

The CAL model provides an alternative approach. Reading assignments typically follow scaffolding activities, so students bring enough prior knowledge to the text to elicit new knowledge from it. One student sums up the benefits:

> As I saw it, the primary purpose of the last class session was to show that learning through reading is just as dependent on prior knowledge as writing. It seems that what is being said is that any book, textbook, or other reading material given to the students must make some "sense" to the students to begin with. The teaching implications of this fact or learning theory are important ... it would seem that what must be done is for the teacher "to make her or his students textbook ready."

APPRENTICES TAKE THE LEAD

In the final third of the course responsibility for learning continues to shift to the apprentice learners, who have assimilated the basic concepts within the course and are engaged in activities in which they decide to accept, modify, expand, or reject the ideas they have encountered.

The students are now engaged in long-term projects, including (1) the ongoing I-Search paper in which each student is investigating a self-selected topic related to language and learning; (2) a five- or eight-week field experience in which students are experimenting with CAL in self-selected practicum sites. The schedule for class time to work on these projects is outlined in the excerpt from the course syllabus shown below.

WRITING RESPONSE GROUPS RETURN

Having already met twice in their writing response groups—first to share topic choice and ask for help locating primary and secondary sources and then to share first drafts—the groups reassemble during the first ninety minutes of Session 11 to continue the process of receiving feedback on the clarity of the current draft. This session provides the kind of peer feedback that will help guide the student-author during revision. Once again the value of heterogeneity becomes clear when observing these groups at work. I typically find that one or two members are more expert with a given topic, others more expert at locating information, and others more expert at "shaping" the language into appropriate language conventions.

EXCERPT FROM COURSE SYLLABUS: SESSIONS 11–15

	11	Writing response groups (revision): support groups	
	12	Writing response groups (editing)	End practicum (option B)
3/3	13	Authors' sharing	Last think/write log due
	14	Practicum panels	I-Search project due
	15	Evaluations; Practicum papers due	Practicum paper due

I make the following suggestions to the students responding to their group members' first drafts:

Purpose: Providing author with feedback to help clarify author's message.

Procedure: Each group member has a copy of author's draft. As author reads draft aloud, members read silently. Each group member takes a turn responding.

Suggested peer responses:

1. Respond first to what is clear:
   "The part that is the clearest to me is _____."
2. Respond next to what is confusing:
   "I'm confused by this sentence. Could you say it another way?"
3. "I would like to know more about _____."

At the end of responses, ask the author what problems she or he is having? The author should come away with ideas for revision of draft that will increase the clarity of the piece.

Group members usually modify the guidelines to meet their preferred way of working. But they remain faithful to the principle of focusing on clarity of ideas at this point rather than the mechanics of language. The students consider the feedback they receive in making their revisions.

It is not surprising to discover college students who have never revised their papers before, as this student so honestly admits:

After reading my "I-Search" paper I still feel unsatisfied. And it's funny, but I feel like it's okay. In a way, I'm afraid or excited to see what my peers will say. As I have stated in the paper, this is the first college paper I have revised for content.

Finally it's time to "shape" the paper for publication. Students meet one more time in their writing response groups; this time they are looking for appropriate language conventions, such as grammatical structure, spelling, and punctuation. The written guidelines are as follows:

Follow the author's lead; let the author indicate areas in which she or he wants help. Do a final check on mechanics, spelling, grammar, and reference forms. Use the APA or MLA style guide. Type the final copy with bibliography and title page.

During this session I bring in reference books (dictionaries, punctuation reminders, etc.). I ask which class members feel comfortable about being identified as "resident editing experts." These students are used as resources when disagreements arise or a group needs clarification of language conventions. I also try to help groups work through problems.

The students consider the feedback they have received and go off to prepare their final drafts.

The group dynamics often change during the writing groups sessions. Because this is the first time many of the students have worked through a transactional piece of writing within a group, there is often a fair amount of the intimidation revealed in this student's log:

> After Thursday's class, I really felt very depressed. First off, I don't particularly care for the way in which we were grouped. I mean nothing is wrong with the members in my writing group, but, I really feel that I am not very helpful to anyone. Andy, Rachael and Debbie know what they are doing and don't seem to need any help whereas, me, I feel like such a fool with them.
>
> Gosh, compared to Andy's writing, my paper is so "Mickey Mouse." How can I help him if I don't know what the lecturer is talking about. I don't dare ask him to write it in easier to understand terms because as he said, "I write for my professor's and not for anyone else."
>
> You would probably comment that I am getting good exposure to different styles of writing, but in actuality I feel so intimidated that I am not learning anything. I dread reading my paper to my group members.

Knowing *what* to do in the group and having a meaningful topic seems to lessen the initial anxiety of novice group members. I have never found all writing groups to work well, but most of them work well most of the time. This student's reaction to the experience is not atypical:

> What is clear now is that students need a clear purpose and audience to make their writing seem more meaningful. They also need to be provided some kind of structure to help them with the process. I see how I will experience this very idea with my own research paper. Sharing my topic with my group members was very helpful. It helped me to clarify exactly what I was trying to find out. Two of the members in my group are experienced teachers and were very helpful as they have worked with my topic (writing groups) and have led me to many resources. I always hear so much about writing groups, and I have a general idea what they are, but I don't really know the theory behind them or their effectiveness with students. I am excited to have the opportunity to research something I have always wanted to know about. I truly understand the importance of having students work on something they are interested in!

WHAT ABOUT THE FINAL PRODUCTS?

The students are to come with their polished drafts next session, prepared to share the highlights orally. Each individual states her or his topic, major finding, and major conclusion, if any, within a three-minute period. Then there is time for questioning the authors. The audiences for these papers are (1) each other and (2) the teacher. The class members then submit their pieces for publication in a class book and each member receives a copy. Expenses are covered by the materials fee for the course.

Class members form a large circle. I suggest to my students that if someone mentions a topic that they are interested in to note who that person is, and consider using that person as a resource. I ask who would like to begin; after a minute of silence, someone volunteers. Sample topics have included "the use of writing groups in the social studies classroom," "invented spelling: an alternative to journal spelling instruction," "collaborative learning: an antithesis to tracking," "schema theory," and "why teach grammar?"

What are the student's responses to "walking through" this process themselves as a way to assimilate the suggested procedures for helping their K–12 students move beyond expressive writing? In the following excerpt, a student points out that this is the first time she has ever shared topics with her classmates. What would Vygotsky say about that?

> It was amazing to see how enthusiastic the *entire* class was about their research paper. Everyone seems to have spent numerous enthusiastic hours in it. I enjoy hearing about the different topics. It really made me aware of how interconnected the reading, writing, discussing & thinking processes are and ways to achieve or initiate these processes.
>
> I was also very pleased that we could share our topics with one another. This was the first time I've experienced this. It made the effort of doing it worth it. That you were able to share your knowledge with others. What a fantastic tool for children to perform. Most of the time children just do work but never get a chance to share their work/knowledge with anyone. The benefits involved in this are numerous for the child as well as for the teacher. Great idea—enjoyed it!

Pride in a "job well done" seems to come across in this college students' log:

> The author sharing was great! When you work hard on something it is nice to be able to share it with others. You are sharing what you found with more people than the teacher. It was so interesting to hear about the great topics others chose and what they found. Everytime I heard a topic that sounded interesting, it motivated me to think—"yeah, that's something I want or need to find out more about." I could see how personal the paper became to the class and how important it was to share ideas/findings. Somehow I think it gave us a feeling of worth. What we worked on was important enough for others to find out and that made me feel really good! Author sharing is a great activity! I could see how many were nervous in the beginning, but once they began to speak about something very near to them, their ideas flowed naturally and easily.

The process in which these learners participated illustrated to them how writers can be guided to move from expressive to transactional writing. Roman shares with us his personal experience with using expressive writing as a basis for transactional pieces:

> . . . the material I write about and make comments about, and relate to, is material I remember. Material I am asked to memorize for a test I tend to

forget. I suspect that most of us are like that—and that is the primary reason why I intend to use a lot of writing in my instruction. And I believe I have learned that expressive writing is essential for good transactional writing to take place later on. Good transactional writing usually reflects writer involvement and understanding of the material he is writing about. Involvement and understanding of material come from expressive writing. 'nuff said.

An I-Search paper is only one example of a long-term project in which students assume greater responsibility for their learning. Besides working on investigative I-Search papers, students may find themselves taking responsibility for writing oral histories, preparing author sharing presentations for peers and parents, producing a play, publishing a newspaper, and so on. In the following box a high school business teacher writes about his students' projects.

K–12 TEACHERS APPLY CAL PRINCIPLES

While teaching, a corporation [was created] in the classroom where fortune cookies were purchased and sold. We created a chart of accounts, sold shares in the company, elected officers, organized the corporate structure, did market, financial, and productivity analysis, sold fortune cookies, made a profit, and distributed the profits after taxes to the students for them to keep. What was interesting was that about a third of the way through, the students began to ask me "Is this for real?" My response was "It's your company to make a profit or loss." The results went beyond what I had hoped for. We sold all the fortune cookies, made a return on investment of 87 percent, and learned much more than what the textbook covered . . . Questions such as "What's the difference between fixed and variable costs?" began to surface. These questions were not introduced during the lesson!
. . . I believe working with a corporation jointly to produce a newsletter for the employees of the company in return for a free lunch at the corporate headquarters would probably make learning even better . . . the revision process could then be implemented in . . . writing.

Many of the ideas for long-term projects emerge from questions students want answered. What might be appropriate projects within your teaching situation?

In this last part of a semester the students carry out long-term projects that require evaluation, synthesis, analysis, and speculation on their part, processes our current literature calls "critical thinking skills." They have been using these processes since their early problem-solving groups, but now they not only have to construct meaning within their groups but also have to help each other develop formal presentations (panels) and share transactional writing pieces with class colleagues and the instructor. They are now almost completely responsible for their own learning. This shift is again reflected in how the class time is used.

HOW MUCH TIME?

The following table shows the time spent in instructor-directed activities (the review) and student-directed activities.

SESSION 11: 180 MINUTES

CAL: Shifting Responsibility	Minutes
Review agenda	15
Writing response groups	90
Practicum support groups	75

PART THREE

IMPLEMENTATION ACROSS THE CURRICULUM

In this part other teachers share their attempts to modify their teaching-learning strategies to reflect more closely the language and learning principles of the CAL model. They describe how they got started, how they coped with problems, and how they came to rethink the teacher-student relationship.

The last chapter addresses issues that arise when teachers are involved in change. The discussion involves curriculum, teacher planning, evaluation, and articulation.

5

TEACHERS IN TRANSITION

WORKING WITH THE CAL TEACHING MODEL

In this chapter both experienced and novice teachers share their attempts to implement teaching strategies compatible with CAL. These are beginning stories from teachers who are willing to risk change because they think it might be beneficial to their students. A sense of professional responsibility to their students seems to drive these teachers to modify their current teaching practices to incorporate current language and learning principles. Taking the first step can be tough, and I appreciate their willingness to share.

These teachers work at various grade levels and in different content areas. Taking the first step included spending time thinking through what might be the major concepts within their course curriculum, in other words, engaging in long-term planning. It may seem rather odd to note long-term planning as a sign of change, but many teachers have not been encouraged to examine their curriculum and make choices about significant and insignificant information. Colleagues and administrators often urge teachers to follow a prescribed commercial program with a teacher's manual.

Having thought through their broad long-term goals, these teachers focused on how to begin with what students already know. With practice they slowly worked their way through the collaborative-apprenticeship process.

BEVERLY: SEVENTH-
AND EIGHTH-GRADE
SOCIAL STUDIES

Beverly has taught school for nine years; currently she teaches American History to approximately 160 seventh- and eighth-grade students. Her classes are ninety minutes long and meet on alternate days. She defines herself as a traditional teacher who "always believed my role to be a transmitter of information." Her dominant mode of instruction was the lecture. We first met in one of my classes, in which, to meet course requirements, Beverly experimented with collaborative-apprenticeship learning (CAL) as an alternative to the traditional teaching model. She continued to experiment with the CAL model. She had just completed her first full year of adapting the model to meet her own needs and the needs of her students when she agreed to participate with me on this project. Beverly shares why she was willing to change:

> Although my Social Studies classes allow for a great deal of discussion, I often found myself lecturing throughout each period and frustrated that my students didn't really seem to comprehend the material taught. The burden of learning always seemed solely my responsibility, but I realized . . . that there should be an eventual shift of this responsibility . . . Feeling guilty that my teaching methods may have led to the negative feelings students developed about writing and language in general as tools of learning, I made the decision to take the risk and use the alternative learning model suggested in the CAL framework. I, myself, learned that language and learning are really inseparable entities which complement each other . . . These beneficial results (to me) . . . encouraged my exploration, evaluation and alteration of my traditional teaching methods.

During the past school year, instead of lecturing and having students read a chapter and answer questions at the end, Beverly began to plan by selecting what she considered to be major concepts within the American history curriculum. She says:

> I've revised my whole curriculum planning and influenced other teachers to experiment with this model. I am more selective of objectives and chapters which I select for discussions. This . . . is more sensible and meaningful than merely covering the enormous quantity of material as demanded by the manual. In being more selective . . . I think I have become more effective.

The following example illustrates the process Beverly used to help her students examine the major causes of the Civil War:

> *Main Objective: Identify the Northern and Southern economic, social and political differences which were the major causes for the Civil War.*

> I began the lesson by asking the students to do a (focused) freewrite on family problems. About 10 minutes later, the class was divided into groups of three and instructed to explore their list of family problems, decide upon the group's two most major concerns and write their two ideas on the board. After each group wrote their contributions, I asked the class to observe similar ties in the lists, and to select the two most recurrent problems . . . My objective here was to identify . . . disagreements among family members as a major problem.

Beverly was starting with her students' frames of reference about conflicts. Their everyday living experiences with their families gave them the background knowledge they needed to undertake this task successfully; collaborating with their peers in small groups gave them the opportunity to pool their knowledge; and sharing the information on the board not only helped make the students' current beliefs public but also gave Beverly student-generated material from which to elicit categories: in this case reasons for family problems, such as "disagreements."

Beverly then connected the results of this class discussion to the course unit entitled "sectional squabbling." She defined family squabbling as fighting among family members. The students identified the North and South as the sections of the United States or family of states who were squabbling during the 1840s. The students returned to their lists of reasons why families disagreed to make predictions about the disagreements between South and North that eventually led to the Civil War.

At this point, Beverly introduced the text chapter entitled, "The Factory Hand and the Slave." She asked the students to read the chapter looking for confirmation of their predictions and to come to class with a chart outlining disagreements between the North and South.

Beverly comments on what happened during the following class session:

> The next class session was a discussion of the chart assignment. I allowed students to collaborate . . . and to present their results . . . on the board. As a class we compared the differences each group identified. I then filled in the missing key points and clarified any questions. The discussion of the differences may take at least two class periods.

This process helped the students use what they already knew about causes for family disagreements to look for similar causes in the family of states that was the United States in the 1840s. They had a "starting point" for undertaking this school task. They could make predictions about the disagreements between North and South; they could read their text looking for confirmation of their predictions; they could begin to list possible causes.

When they returned to class, the students first had the opportunity to collaborate with peers. In small problem-solving groups they shared their individual predictions and noted areas of consensus and differences.

Students were expected to use the text (and other references) as evidence to support their viewpoints.

The small groups shared their results with the whole class by putting their information on the board. Beverly and class members compared the differences in the student-generated information; she filled in the gaps and responded to questions.

Sometimes Beverly used written logs instead of answering the students' questions orally.

> At the end of each class period, I allow a few minutes for oral summaries of the day's lesson or I ask for a written log to determine whether they understood the material covered. The students could write questions in the log or ask them in class.

Beverly also used a written project rather than an examination for her primary evaluation of her students' understanding. The process she used included peer writing groups. She provided two class sessions in which peers met in their writing groups to provide each other with feedback on their essays in progress. She did not grade these drafts. The following excerpts are from an essay in which the students identified differences between the North and South that contributed to the causes of the Civil War. The first excerpt is an eighth-grader's early draft; the second (following the handwritten draft) is the final draft turned in for a grade.

The first draft received feedback by the student's peers in a writing response group, which guided her revisions. Beverly did not evaluate this early draft.

First draft

But there were ~~som~~ some ways they were similar. They both treated the blacks and immigrants in the same way. Immigrants weren't treated as ~~It~~ bad as blacks but they were victims of racial discrimination. Also they both benifited from Eli Whitney's cotton gin. It boosted industry + it boosted cotton growing and something that the North didn't ~~inta~~ intend it boosted slavery.

     So ~~tott~~ the differences overbalanced the similarities. This made the separation of the North and South even greater.

Final draft

The separation between North and South was due partially to unwillingness to change ideas and opinions to compromise. The result was the outbreak of hostilities well known as the Civil War. One of the major differences that contributed to the growth of the division was the competitive attitude of the two economies. Both North and South defined economy as a way of making profits by producing the finished product with the least expense for labor.

The North believed that industry and business was better than the Southerners' farming and plantations. The South, of course, had exactly the opposite opinion.

Certain developments benefited both North and South but set the separation wedge even deeper. Two of these were inventions of one man: Eli Whitney. Whitney's factory system, an assembly line in which workers produced many products piece by piece, was used by the North. Whitney's cotton gin, a machine that cleaned staple-cotton (a kind of crop) quickly, was used by the South. The Northern economy benefited from the factory system. When businessmen needed more workers for their factories, they hired immigrants for lower wages than Americans would accept. The cotton gin boosted the cotton industry in the South. The cotton gin worked so quickly that the South needed more and more cotton. So they bought slaves so they wouldn't have to pay wages and could acquire even more profits.

As the economic competition grew between North and South it divided them more and more. So the differences in their economic systems contributed to the separation of America.

Beverly allowed her students to begin with what they know, helped them build on that knowledge, and gave them opportunities to develop the connections they were making in expressive writing (logs and first drafts) and exploratory talk with their peers. In several instances, the students developed their language and thinking with the help of peer writing response groups. These transactional writing pieces reflected students' internalization of ideas and their control over the appropriate language conventions needed to express those ideas.

Beverly reports an unexpected benefit as she found herself moving toward the role of learner:

> By allowing the students to have more peer interaction and to have them share their findings with the class, I found myself more able to be an observer of how learning was taking place. As an observer, I could then modify some of the activities and improve on the results I hope to achieve.

One of those observations led Beverly and her colleagues to change from homogeneous to heterogeneous classes. She discovered the educational benefits of using problem-solving small groups made up of members with varied life experiences and interests; the language and thinking coming from these heterogeneous groups appeared to her to be more complex.

Beverly considers herself now to be a teacher-learner, a professional who will continue to modify her teaching as she gains in knowledge and expertise. In her words, "I feel like a novice teacher in some ways because I have new tools which I need to become more experienced at using. I am challenged with a new insight into teaching and learning."

HAUNANI: UNIVERSITY FOREIGN LANGUAGE

Haunani, a guest speaker for one of my undergraduate classes, shared how she experimented with the CAL model when she returned to the classroom to teach beginning Hawaiian to a group of eighteen university students. Her class was made up primarily of young men who had never studied a foreign language. The fifty-five-minute class met Monday through Friday for one semester.

Haunani's goals for her students were to have them use Hawaiian language for meaningful purposes and real audiences, not just to take tests. In her previous teaching experiences she had emphasized drill and practice as her primary teaching strategies.

On the first day of class she asked her students to engage in a focused freewrite activity. Using expressive writing, they responded to these questions: "What do you know about the Hawaiian language?" "What would you like to know about the language?" and "What are the goals you set for yourself in this class?" The students would keep their freewrites throughout the semester to monitor how well their goals were being met.

After doing the freewrites the students met in randomly chosen small groups to share their responses to the questions. The small groups then shared the results of their discussions with the whole class by writing the major points on chart paper, which was put up on the walls. The process made public what this community of learners knew about the Hawaiian language and gave both students and instructor a foundation on which to build.

During this early part of the course, Haunani's relationship with her students was asymmetrical because she set up most of the scaffolding activities. Everything she said in the classroom was in Hawaiian; she tried to keep the language connected to the concrete scaffolding activities in which she and the students were engaged.

The students sang songs and learned a hula; she wrote class letters in Hawaiian tied to upcoming holidays like Valentine's and St. Patrick's Days; and guest speakers talked about and demonstrated various parts of the Hawaiian culture.

Students collaborated in small groups for a variety of purposes. For example, they worked together on homework assignments in which they tried to figure out appropriate Hawaiian language structures; their home-work responses were shared in class on chart paper. Haunani confirmed appropriate responses and pointed out how she viewed the incorrect re-sponses as logical hypotheses on the part of the students. Of the peer collaboration, she said, "The small group discussions were my favorite part . . . the students talked . . . I tried not to talk unless they asked something directly."

She also used think/write logs as another vehicle for discovering areas of confusion. Students wrote on a weekly basis. Most used English, but from midsemester to the end of the course a few wrote in Hawaiian. Haunani told my undergraduate class:

> By the time they were using think/write logs they weren't afraid to express their feeling; they gave me hell about the mid-term exam . . . too hard . . . When I thought it was appropriate, I would compile comments (from the logs), type them up and give them back; sometimes these went up on the wall.

Increasingly the students worked in collaborative small groups, the vehicle Haunani used to shift responsibility to the novices. In the last four weeks of the course, the students' goals were (1) to comprehend the ideas in the final chapter of their Hawaiian language text and (2) to complete a long-term writing project.

Haunani relinquished formal lessons. Students worked with partners to help each other clarify and expand each other's understanding of the text. They worked with a partner or in a small writing response group to help them through the revision and editing process of their individual projects, which were books written in Hawaiian.

The students were responsible for organizing their time to carry out these tasks. In Haunani's words:

... they set up a calendar which outlined on this day we are going to do this [and so forth] ... a copy of the calendar was given to me. At the end of every day, they wrote a think/write log in which they responded to the problems of the day . . . Were you successful? How do you know? Were you not successful? How do you know? What is the evidence and how do you feel about it? We had this ongoing log of their progress. They had the option of coming to class or not. They all came. I had perfect attendance. When they needed me to fill in gaps, I was there.

During the writing process Haunani discovered that some of her students started to write drafts of their book in English and then tried to translate these pieces into Hawaiian. These students discovered it would be better if they thought and wrote in Hawaiian. Haunani says, ". . . that wasn't something I could tell them."

Since the students had previous experience in this class with revising and editing when they wrote thank-you notes to their guest speakers and invitations to the upcoming Authors' Party, they weren't afraid to scratch out and revise their drafts. Finally the day came when the books were finished; invited guests arrived and the student authors read their "published" pieces to their audience.

Evaluation of student progress took several forms. Haunani included quizzes, a midterm examination, a final examination, the "published" book, observation of students use of Hawaiian with guest speakers, and the student-written log responses on how well they had met their own goals.

Haunani says that in the collaborative student-teacher relationship, ". . . they mold me; and I mold them . . . it's no longer only teacher's needs but students' needs as well."

She ended her discussion with my undergraduate class with a written postscript that includes her thoughts on her first experience with the collaborative-apprenticeship process. In addition to meeting her goal of having her students use the Hawaiian language for meaningful purposes and real audiences, she wrote the following five statements:

1. I used the framework because it's consistent with my ideas and observations; it's also consistent with Hawaiian culture, particularly where group work is involved.

2. Implementing the framework took a lot of time, especially in the areas of soul-searching and planning, but it was worth it.

3. We used some aspects of the framework more than others, and, more often than not, the process was recursive as opposed to being linear.

4. There was learning at many different levels:

   a. Students learning Hawaiian grammar.

   b. Student reflecting on their own goals and learning styles.

   c. Students interacting with each other.

   d. Students interacting with Haunani both as a group and as individuals.

e. Haunani learning about each student via think/write logs.

f. Haunani learning more about the framework.

g. Others (visitors, students & teachers from other classes) learning about our class.

5. I would use the framework again.

As Haunani did in statement 1, a number of other teachers experimenting with CAL mentioned its appropriateness for multicultural classrooms. Her statements 2 and 3 reflect the flexibility of the CAL model. Adapting the framework—particularly the strategies—to meet the needs of one's teaching situation is typical and desirable. What is important to remember is the collaborative-apprenticeship learning model itself and its underlying language and learning principles.

Evidence of Haunani viewing herself as teacher/learner is present in statements e and f. Statement b illustrates another dimension of encouraging students to take more responsibility for their own learning. In the literature, this process of reflecting on what one is doing is often known as using metacognitive strategies. In other words, being conscious of their learning strategies gives students knowledge of the tools they can use to plan their approach to problems.

ANNA: THIRD-GRADE MATH

Anna has taught in both public and private elementary schools for thirteen years. She is currently teaching first grade. Anna's first years in the teaching profession left her feeling uncomfortable.

As a K-1 teacher, teaching children how to read through phonics workbooks and worksheets was a grueling process for many students. I was laden with guilt when I authoritatively set a minimum number of worksheet pages to do before anyone could go out to recess. Whenever a child moaned or got confused over the many different sounds of the short vowels, I battled with frustration wondering if there was a better way to teach this. I began to question many of the practices in the suggested curriculum. Phonics in isolation was not meaningful for the children and the majority of the children were not motivated to do the workbook and worksheets. It was mainly done because it was a "rule" to do your work.

She was uncomfortable enough to decide to teach only half-time and go back to school. Anna wanted to figure out how to motivate children to learn, but she found herself examining how *she* learned. Thinking of her own positive and negative previous school experiences, she remembers first the memorable and then the painful:

. . . being in my high school speech class debating the pros and cons of different birth control techniques in a small group of two boys and four girls.

... playing a game in a high school economics class where each student had to trade and barter chips of differing values relative to the theory of supply and demand.

... my kindergarten teacher who loved my tempera painting of patterned lines and dots so much that she wanted to put it in the school office. (We had been learning about patterns using colored wooden beads and blocks. Apparently, she was thrilled that I had transferred the idea to a painting!)

These were the memorable moments. I have a list of painful memories as well.

... my first grade teacher who had gray hair, gold-rimmed bifocal spectacles which she peered over from the top of her nose ... and who had little patience. With a well oiled, wooden yardstick in hand, she sat 15 children on the floor in a circle to do round robin style reading. We read a paragraph at a time about Dick, Jane and Spot. If we did not keep our place as to where the person before us had just read, we got a mean scowl, an angry complaint about not paying attention and a whack on the thigh or hand with that yardstick. I was petrified and a 6 year old nervous wreck!

... a Human Development professor who lectured so far above our heads and based her exams solely on textbook readings and lectures, 23 out of 25 students received a "D" on their first mid-term.

As Anna explains, her memorable activities held some meaning for her and were carried out in a nonthreatening environment that allowed her to take risks. Both of these elements were missing in her painful school memories.

Anna began to become more conscious of the similarities between what had motivated her to learn in earlier school experiences and what was working for her in her current university studies. She discovered that meaningful tasks and classes in which she felt she could take risks continued to motivate her to learn.

At this point Anna began considering how she might change as a teacher. How could she use what she now knew about how *she* learned to facilitate the learning of her students? Looking for a teaching model to modify or replace the traditional teacher as examiner, Anna decided to experiment with the CAL model.

In Anna's half-time position she was teaching math to third graders. Her first attempt to implement ideas from the CAL model began after the school year had already started. She decided that she could change the teaching-learning strategies she used and still follow the ongoing curriculum. In the next several pages, she describes how she introduced these third graders to fractions.

Basically, the first step was that they needed to learn that a fraction is a part of a whole and that it could be expressed in a mathematical form. They would only be learning simple fractions such as 1/2, 1/4, 3/4, etc. When the math period began, I asked the class to fold a piece of binder paper lengthwise in half. On the left hand side, they were to label it "before" and on the right hand side, "after."

In order to elicit student prior knowledge of fractions, I wrote on the board, "What is 1/6?" I asked them to write (under the "before" column) whatever they could about "1/6." That didn't take very long. With a quick walk around the class, most of them did not know *anything* about fractions. They kept asking me, "What *is* one sixth?" Most of them had only written the question, "What is 1/6?" on their paper and that was that. However, two boys had known what was 1/6!

I thought, aha! I can get a discussion going using those two. The boys described it as being "1/6 of something." Most of the class was still quiet yet and they merely listened to what Bobby and Gary had to say.

I asked for examples of what they meant. Gary, who is generally quiet and rarely spoke up in class explained that "If you had six cubes and you took one of them, that was one sixth."

I brought out a box of multicolored wooden cubes and asked him to demonstrate what he had talked about. In the meantime, Bobby kept a close watch on Gary.

I pointed to the examples of fractions on the board and asked if they could use the cubes to show what was meant (like what Bobby and Gary had done), then make up some of their own fractions. Each box had approximately 50 cubes.

There was a great deal of discussion and everyone got a chance to experience making their own fractions. Some of them wanted to do 1/100, 1/1000, 1/1,000,000, etc. They were using their imaginations and were extending and applying the concept. Great!

Then I asked them to regroup for another activity:

Two groups with six children

Two groups with four children

One group with three children

One group with two children

Then I took out a tray of round danish pastries. Everyone's eyes bulged, tongues began licking lips, and there were many "yumms!"

I had 8" x 10" cue cards with 1/2, 1/3, 1/4, and 1/6 written on each card. I asked them which fraction they thought was the largest. Since the first activity dealt with cubes of equal sizes, most of them naturally thought that 1/6 was the largest, since that would have the most cubes and it was the largest number. I said we'd find out.

I emphasized that each child would be getting a fraction of each pastry. I gave each group a pastry placed on a paper plate along with some napkins. I gave each group a fraction cue card depending on the number of children in each group. That is, the group with six had the fraction 1/6, the group of four had the fraction 1/4, the group of three had 1/3, etc.

I went to each group and sliced the pastry according to the number of children sitting in the group, each time emphasizing that I wanted each of them to get an equal share.

Immediately, they began wanting to switch groups. But somehow, the two in the 1/2 group sat firmly in their seats, not wanting to move.

Somehow though, they were each happy to have a slice of pastry no matter how small. I guess it tasted so good. After our little surprise snack, I collected the cue cards and taped them to the blackboard and illustrated each fraction accordingly.

We talked about which fraction was the largest and why. There were all kinds of generalizations:

"The larger the bottom number is, the smaller the size of each piece."

"You always say the bottom number with "th" except for 1/2 and 1/3."

"When you divide the pie in slices, the pieces all have to be equal."

New questions were also asked:

"What if you have a "2" or "3" on the top instead of just "1"?

"Why do you have to draw the line in the middle?"

Next I passed out a prediction guide that showed pictures of four people eating a pizza, three children sharing a granola bar, and two boys eating a sandwich. I asked them to predict and show how each item would be divided equally, how it would be written and how it would be said.

They wrote their answers out and shared the answers with their small group. They discussed similarities and clarified misunderstandings. The fascinating thing was that their reasoning was being verbalized. For the first time I was relieved that there was much talking and learning going on in the class, and I was enjoying it!

The last ten minutes of the class were spent on their learning logs—the "after" part of their folded sheets of paper.

I asked them to answer "What is 1/6?" and to explain as much as they could about what they had done and learned. Secondly, I asked them to write on anything they were confused about and [said] that I would write back to them if they had any questions.

This was their first time writing about math and many of them were stumped. Some said, "I know everything already." Some could only write numbers. So I asked them to make believe they were explaining what 1/6 was to their mothers. How would you explain it? Write it down as if you were actually saying it.

There were still some looks of frustration. Then I spotted Jessica and Jan's writing. They had drawn a picture of a pie divided up in pieces and explained what their picture meant. I asked them if they were willing to share their logs with the others. They were glad to and read what they had written to the rest of the class. It was not very long, but it was a start and a model for the others. It gave them the idea of putting math into writing. Slowly, the "Oh. . . ," "I see," "Now I get it," began popping up and more pencils began moving.

The lessons went on:

What is a numerator and denominator?

What does 2/3 mean?

What is 1/3 of 15?

Is 1/2 = 4/8? Why or why not?

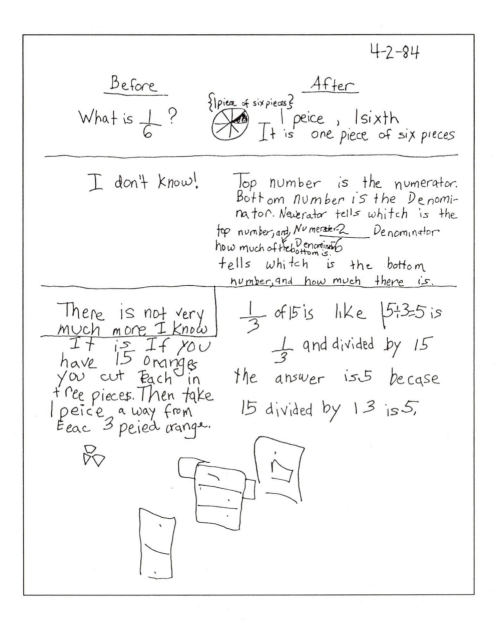

I started each day with students each writing a question on their "before" side of their paper, and an answer (learning logs) on the "after" side as shown in the example above.

Concrete experiences were heavily needed as they had very little prior knowledge about fractions.

By the end of the chapter, I had realized that the more opportunity I gave them to talk, the more they were able to comprehend, retain, and apply. With more concrete experiences, there was more discussion and writing.

Anna's first attempt at implementing the collaborative-apprenticeship learning process was several years ago. Since then she has changed schools and now has her own first-grade classroom again. She has continued to modify her teaching-learning practices and to examine the content itself, shifting toward a more integrated curriculum. She is consciously making room for her students' own goals, as noted in the example of her integrated language arts and science unit about the ocean (described in Chapter 3). She incorporates student interest into her planning by taking into consideration what they already know and what they want to know. Typical questions that her first-grade students wanted answers to included:

What's the biggest whale in the world?

What's the largest shark in the world?

Can you eat a shark?

What do sharks eat?

Do hammerhead sharks eat people?

This fascination with sharks and other sea creatures is also present in Elizabeth and Anne's integrated curriculum.

ELIZABETH AND ANNE: KINDERGARTEN SCIENCE

Elizabeth had been teaching kindergarten for four years; Anne had taught preschool for five. They decided to collaborate on possible ways to implement the CAL model in Elizabeth's kindergarten class of twenty-six students.

Working within an integrated science curriculum they chose a number of major concepts that they wanted to share with their students. This part of the science curriculum uses the ocean as the underlying theme from which various topics emerge. Since these children live in Hawaii, issues related to the ocean arise daily. The long-term plan that guided Anne and Elizabeth's teaching strategies and choice of materials is shown on the opposite page.

In Appendix 2 Elizabeth and Anne share with us the strategies they used in week 3, when they worked with the children on the concept "Sea creatures protect themselves in many different ways." Instead of using focused freewriting as a technique for finding out what the students already know about this subject, these teachers used the "think-pair-share" procedure. In this procedure the teacher poses a question to the whole class (in this case, "What are some of the different ways animals in the sea protect themselves?").

PRACTICUM

Major
concept: The Amazing Diversity of Sea Creatures

Sub-
concepts: Week 1: Sea creatures come in many sizes and shapes
                       which help them to do many things.

              Week 2: Sea creatures move in many different ways.

              Week 3: Sea creatures protect themselves in many
                       different ways.

              Week 4: Ocean animals eat in food chains.

              Week 5: There are differences between marine mammals
                       and fishes.

              Week 6: Sea Creatures live in many different homes
                       called habitats.

              Week 7: Sharks are different from other fish. There
                       are many different kinds of sharks (that may
                       vary by size, shape, food they eat, and way
                       they bear their young).

The children think silently for one to two minutes. At the teacher's signal, the children find a partner nearby and share what they know for three to five minutes. During the pair sharing, the teachers move among the pairs facilitating the sharing through active-listening and modeling if necessary. At the teacher's signal, the children and teachers reassemble in the large group to share what they talked about and learned.

What was the benefit of using this procedure rather than freewriting or brainstorming? At this age the teachers felt that talk would be a more appropriate way to begin, although they later included drawing and writing. They chose the think-pair-share over brainstorming because

> it was more directed and flowed into the next step of making public what students know . . . Using this procedure . . . provided a consistent activity for collaboration and helped to make the children feel secure in a regular routine.

Anne and Elizabeth observed that initially the kindergartners felt strange about being given the opportunity to share with their peers, but the idea of collaboration eventually took hold:

> . . . children began their sharing with "We talked about how" and "We thought that" . . . I found this behavior very significant since children at kindergarten level are still usually very egocentric in their thinking . . . What a nice way to incorporate social skills . . . at an early age!!

The teachers used the student-generated information as a foundation for building knowledge. They confirmed children's hypotheses and expanded on them by showing pictures of animals protecting themselves. They also introduced vocabulary terms like *defend, poison,* and *electricity* within the context of confirming the children's guesses. Nine forms of protection came out of the children's sharing: poison, biting, tricks, pinching, hiding, swimming, size, electricity, and talk.

Their second scaffolding activity involved dividing the students up into small groups to work on dramatizing some of the various forms of protection. Some children used role-playing to show dolphins "talking" to each other to warn of the approach of an enemy. Such concrete activities were effective scaffolding activities. Elizabeth notes that "Activities involving movement such as role-playing and active games helped to reinforce the learning through play. Play is the natural way a young child learns . . ."

Finally Elizabeth and Anne asked the children to choose their favorite sea creature, draw a picture of it, and guess its form of protection. When the children had finished with their drawings, they reassembled to share their information and place their pictures on a large chart under categories they made up; finally the teachers labeled the child-created categories.

In this process the children have shared publicly what they already knew about the topic. The teachers confirmed their background knowledge and introduced additional information via pictures and role-playing. Then they helped the children develop categories for sea creatures with the same means of protecting themselves.

Next Anne and Elizabeth introduced literature into the curriculum: in this case Leo Lionni's 1963 book *Swimmy.* They asked the children to predict what sea animals and what forms of defense would be found in the book. Then they read the book to the children.

Elizabeth and Anne decided to use think/write logs so students could write what they learned and at the same time collaborate with the teacher by using expressive writing. Of course writing at this age level overlaps with drawing as a means of communication. In fact the directions to the children were "Draw a sea creature and tell about the way it protects itself." The students were prepared for this use of drawing/writing beforehand when the teachers showed examples of logs on an overhead projector. Elizabeth and Anne experimented with how to respond to the logs.

> In the initial logs we copied each child's writing below their own [invented spelling] . . . and explained "This is the way what you wrote would look like in print." But we felt we were doing language experience and defeating our primary purpose for writing . . . clarifying and communicating areas of confusion. After making the decision to switch to responding to the child's ideas and/or responding with a question about their ideas, we felt more collaboration was taking place. The children enjoyed reading our responses.

They did not grade the logs but wrote responses to the messages. These logs provide an interesting example of the development of language and thinking as a by-product of problem-solving activities. Michael's logs show his writing development. During week 1 he is using drawing exclusively to convey his message; by week 7 invented spelling dominates.

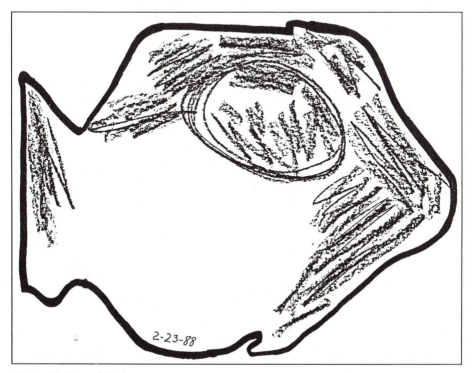

Michael's Log: Week 1

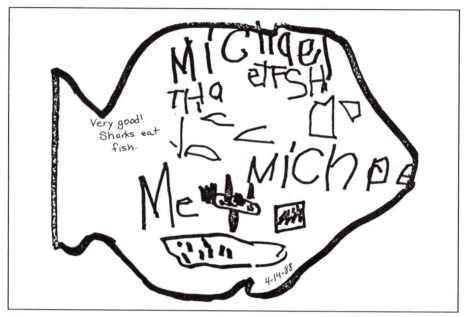

Michael's Log: Week 7

Leilani's logs illustrate her development of the sentence structure "I can see . . ."

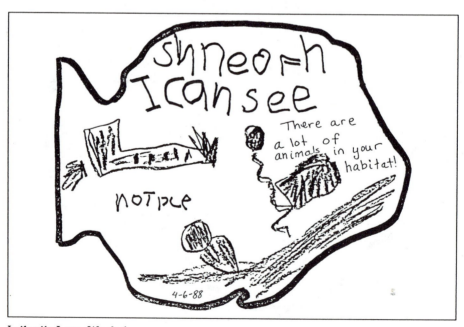

Leilani's Log: Week 6

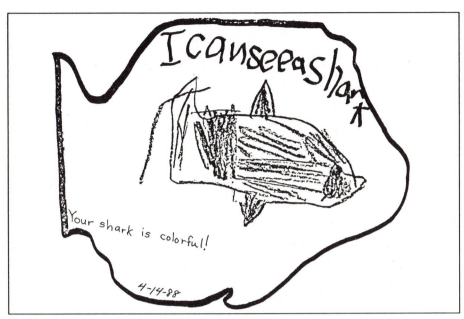

Leilani's Log: Week 7

Michelle moves from making a list to writing sentences.

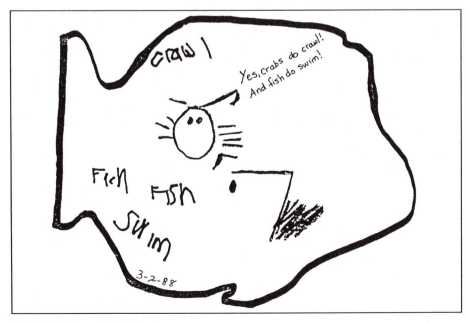

Michelle's Log: Week 2

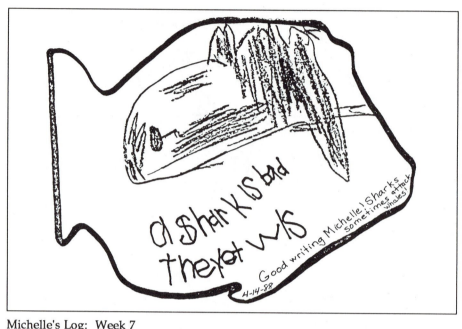

Michelle's Log: Week 7

For their final activity, these children prepared for a trip to Sea Life Park. In Elizabeth's own words:

> Many children had never been there before and were thrilled beyond belief to see and experience the concepts we had covered in class. It was the most meaningful trip these children had been on all year. They were enthralled with recognizing live hammerhead sharks and were able to point out some of their special characteristics, such as their gills and scaly covering. This type of discovery and affirmation of learning went on throughout the course of the field trip. An additional . . . benefit for all the teachers was that there were few behavior problems. The children were so busy making connections with what we studied that they had little time for diversions such as misbehaving.

SUMMARY

The educational contexts in which these teachers work varies. The instructors all molded the CAL model to fit the purposes, audiences, and conventions of their different disciplines. But they tried to remain true to collaborative-apprenticeship learning. They tried to start with what the students knew, share that knowledge, build on it collaboratively, use language as a tool for learning, and support increasing student initiative.

Of course they faced problems. The next chapter describes some of the problems that occurred as teachers switched to the CAL model, and the solutions they generated.

6

PROBLEMS AND SOLUTIONS

ADAPTING CAL TO YOUR TEACHING SITUATION

Change is not easy. It takes time and practice and lots of support from others. The first attempts of the teachers quoted in this chapter often failed. But these teachers continued to experiment until they figured out how to modify and adapt CAL notions to fit their needs and the needs of their students while remaining true to the model's underlying language and learning principles. In the following section teachers describe what happened when they tried out various CAL strategies.

STARTING WHERE THE STUDENTS ARE

In order to help students expand their knowledge, teachers need to know what that knowledge is. This second grader provides a clue as he responds to a focused freewrite question about families:

What is a Family?

A Family is a big bunch of people.

Sharon teaches a fifth-grade class at a private school. She tried focused freewriting as a strategy to elicit student knowledge.

> The freewriting activity proved troublesome at first. Students feared being graded on what they did NOT know. The fifth grade is the first year letter grades are utilized and implemented. Therefore, students see every activity as one that may significantly affect their grades. Students became very apologetic at first ("I'm sorry I don't know anything about King Lot"), but a few, while apologizing, did attempt to ask questions so as to follow the instructions of "keep writing until I say stop". . . .
>
> The focused freewriting activity became more successful as students began to grow aware of the fact that I was not grading them. They seemed to feel free to take risks with their prior knowledge . . . the students really did not mind expressing their ideas or opinions once the fear of grading was erased from their minds.
>
> Having clear and specific questions and directions also proved important. Since the framework was a new concept being worked on by both the teacher and the students, it was essential that I be very precise with my directions to avoid problems with student understanding.

Lori tells a similar story with her introduction of writing as a tool for learning in her seventh-grade English class.

> First of all, the freewriting sessions for the first 3–4 weeks did not go very well. A few students picked up right away but I found that they were students who had experienced freewriting in the past. I think the main reason it did not work in the beginning was because it was a new experience for most of them. The first step was to assure them that I was not going to look at spelling, grammar, etc. Students were still clutching their white out bottles and erasers and using them! I had to remind them that they did not need it and to just cross out anything they wanted to change. When we got past that stage, they went to the extreme opposite direction and wrote so illegibly that I could not decipher their writing! . . . Also if students did not have much prior knowledge on the subject they refused to try to write more on the topic besides "I do not know anything about _____ ." Part of the problem could also have been that my questions were too focused so they felt there had to be a right or wrong answer rather than just expressing their ideas.
>
> Gradually, however, the freewriting began to work and became very useful. I found this especially true when I started my mythology unit. By this point students knew what to expect from the freewriting and were much more comfortable with it. I found that taking their freewriting and sharing it in their groups to come up with a prediction on the definition of mythology worked very well. Those who had very little prior knowledge had other group members who had information to contribute so there was not a lot of pressure on them. Also those who did have a strong background were very proud as they were the "group experts" on the subject. One student who resisted freewriting all along wrote a very impressive list in his freewrite and provided very valuable input orally to his group definition of mythology.

My thology

Zeus
Hera
appolo
Mercury (Hermes)
Mars
pluto
Hades
Medusa
Bellorophan
pegasus
crete
athens
Mycane
Hercules
Hydra
River of Styx
acchilles
poseidon

oddy see
wooden hoarse
Troy
arcadia
Fathon
Hephestus
Venus
aphrodite
cupid
pan
Midas
Hundred eyed augus

I have had mythology at lincoln
But I used to read when
I was in 4 to 5 grade

This really showed me how useful freewriting can be for students who resist writing in paragraphs . . . listing can also be a very useful tool in (eliciting) prior knowledge. I think this activity motivated this student to demonstrate his knowledge in the following lessons and the students truly looked upon him as an "expert." It was a great confidence builder for this student who was otherwise known as a "troublemaker." The freewriting helped me because it showed the diverse prior knowledge students possessed at the start of the unit.

Linda, an experienced elementary school teacher, decided to try CAL in her social studies block of time. The school year had already started and the curriculum was in place. Linda began the process of rethinking her teaching strategies before she introduced her students to the next unit, "European Explorers." She "started off with a focused freewrite asking the students to tell me what they think an explorer is and to name their favorite explorer. I did this to elicit their prior knowledge . . . about explorers."

Writing freewrite questions that are neither so broad that the students don't know how to begin to answer them or so narrow that only students with specialized knowledge can respond takes some practice, as Linda discovered.

One of my biggest problems I had at the beginning of CAL was creating meaningful questions for the focus freewrites. One of my biggest bombs was when I asked the class to compare the Spanish explorers with the British explorers. They just did not have enough prior knowledge even though it seemed obvious to me from the text. My most successful questions were those directly related to personal experiences in their lives. For instance, probably a better question for my first focus freewrite might have been, "Have you ever explored anything? What was it like?" rather than "What is an explorer?" There is an art to questioning and I am much more conscious of how to use questions to initiate a discussion now.

But once the students have some experience with freewriting and understood its purpose, the benefits become clearer. Alan, teaching a high school English literature class found that "Once the students became used to the mode of freewriting, they were able to write without worrying about mechanics. I found that many students who were quiet and seemed to be 'somewhere else' had many things to say in writing."

Indeed, how many teachers would have guessed what this quiet elementary student knew about the military?

Western command is Hawaii Ft. Shaffer. 25 Infantry division is in Hawaii. There are 24 divisions in the U. S. Airforce inlisted men ranks. 1. airman 2. airman First Class 3. Senior air man 4. Sergenant 5. Staff sergenant 6. Technical Sergeant 7. Master serganant 8. Senior master sergeant 9. Chief master sergent. Officers in the air force. 1. second Lieutenant 2. First Lieutenant 3. Captain 4. Major 5. Lieutenant Colonel 6. Colonel 7. Brigadier general 8. Major general 9. Lieutenant general 10. general. Army inlested men 1. private 2. private First class 3. Corporal 4. sergeant 5. staff sergenant 6. Platoon sergeant

It was hard because I had a lot to write. It was easy because I new most of it. The reason for that is my dad is in the reserve! Also because I watch miltary shows. Finaly I like to read about it.

While most teachers in our discussions examined the role of freewriting as a strategy to elicit prior knowledge, this does not negate the importance of brainstorming and drawing as alternative techniques.

COLLABORATIVE
SMALL GROUPS

Because of the underlying CAL principle that learning is inherently social in origin, peer collaboration is encouraged throughout this teaching-learning model. My university students collaborate with each other on the first day of class to pool their background knowledge about topic x. But whether sharing prior knowledge on a given subject, working to clarify the text, or engaging in long-term tasks in peer writing groups, problems seem to arise when students do not have a clear understanding of the purpose of the group task, the task holds little meaning for them, or they have had little experience with working in problem-solving groups and don't understand their roles.

What I have started to do in my university classes is to take about forty minutes to set the stage, so to speak. My students respond to the freewrite questions: "What are some problems that could come up during group work that could interfere with the group working together well?" "What are some possible solutions?" They write responses to the first question for about fifteen minutes. They meet in groups of three; each member reads aloud his or her response to the first question while the others listen for similarities and differences; and they compile their results. This process is repeated for the second question. Finally one member from each group shares the group results with the whole class. I try to make connections between the various groups' ideas on problems and solutions. Now we have student-generated lists of possible problems in group work and possible solutions. The students are responsible for implementing their solutions, and when necessary I am available as a mediator.

A number of teachers use this same process in lower grades, but they write the problems and solutions on large chart paper and put it on a wall where students and teacher alike can refer to it.

Giving specific directions early in the year, when students may be truly novices with group work, also seems to be helpful because it helps students begin their task and provides guidance for completing the task. Linda writes about her experience with some groups in her fifth-grade class:

> The collaboration was very successful, especially after I learned how to initiate group work. I gave very precise instructions and I gave the students a time period to work in. This kept them on task. I also had one student record the consensus and then had the group present their findings.

Even with a clear understanding of the task and a conducive environment, it usually takes time and practice. As one high school teacher acknowledges, "students had trouble at first [but] with practice and some modeling, students learned to focus their talk on the subject."

This same teacher pointed out the benefits of regular talk in small groups for ESL students. For these students who were learning English, "The talk helped develop their language, fostered social interaction, and provided them (ESL students) with immediate feedback. It allowed students to use each other as resources to clarify, confirm, and expand ideas."

The three teachers quoted below discovered the benefits of using heterogeneous groups for peer collaboration.

1. There is more peer interaction in my classroom. Students are given more opportunities to collaborate and express themselves. In science, for example, students are given the opportunity to work in

groups to discuss a term definition, find a solution to a problem, or collect data. Because the students are heterogeneously grouped, peer interaction is very beneficial to all.

2. Another valuable step [after reading] is small group discussion. Allow the students time to collaborate with each other. This is a very helpful means of expressing, clarifying and organizing their thoughts . . . This simple exchange of ideas often bridges the gap between "Huh?" and "Now I get it!" Students of different backgrounds and experiences are an invaluable resource for their peers.

3. My students have greatly benefited from collaboration. The shy ones have opened up and the leaders have come to realize that they really do NOT know everything! They have learned to like each other on a different level . . . they have come to appreciate and respect each other.

Karen's elementary students express their own opinions toward peer collaboration in their think/write logs. Sometimes the reaction focused on what was learned.

It was best with a group from the begining, but then I finished it up alone. It was nice to work together. We all learned tha most of it was recyclable. We also learned what are the things we used to make our pictures.

Sometimes the reaction focused on what was felt.

It was alot esere to do it with someone because I needed alot more than just matiral. Thats why I needed someone to do it with. And I really liked it alot. because it was fun and I like being with someone I like because sometimes I feel lonely or sad.

BUILDING ON
PRIOR KNOWLEDGE

Having elicited student knowledge on a given topic, a number of teachers had some difficulty deciding what to do next. Thinking through possible scaffolding activities takes time and practice. The activities illuminate an underlying course concept in such a way that students can make connections between the new ideas and their background knowledge. First tries don't always work. Sue, an elementary teacher, shares a first attempt. Both the frustration and the optimism can be seen in the following excerpt.

> After eliciting prior knowledge [on America], I didn't know how to make a connection to [the concept] "how [the topic choice] contributed to the growth of their country"... I knew that I was not clear myself what I wanted to do because the children did question when they didn't make any sense of what America had to do with the topic of their choice. It was then that I decided that I needed to focus on one of my objectives and not try to accomplish so much at one time. It definitely was a learning experience for me. The children taught me that, and I had to change the lesson as we went along. The children saw that the teacher makes mistakes too.

Sharon emphasizes the need for thinking through appropriate scaffolding activities. The scaffolding needs to build on what the students already know. With novices it might be necessary to use everyday knowledge demonstrated in some concrete fashion to illustrate the concept being introduced. Sharon writes about scaffolding ideas from her fifth-grade science curriculum.

> Appropriate scaffolding experiences are wonderful to the learning process! Utilizing creative dramatic activities, field trips, guest speakers and films, for example, proved very beneficial. I found that those activities where the students were actively involved proved highly effective... For example, to introduce the concept of "rotation and revolution," I had students involved in a creative movement activity where they rotated as the earth does. They then moved around the "sun." The "sun" was the student, in each group of five, wearing yellow . . . the students quickly grasped the concepts involved ... [in their learning logs] several chose to describe what they had learned in a visual manner. Their illustrations demonstrated the very movements we performed as a class.

That's one example of using a student activity as part of a scaffolding structure very early in the semester. Once the teacher and students have worked out a starting point, they can build on it by making connections between each successive activity. As apprentice learners assimilate basic concepts, the scaffolding changes form, moving from concrete demonstrations to concrete examples. Finally students have built up enough shared knowledge that they can rely increasingly on exchanging ideas through written and oral dialogue alone. At this point much of the specialized vocabulary specific to a particular discipline has become part of the students' vocabulary.

Is it worth it to take the time to think through scaffolding activities for novices? Renee shares in a log how she used the memory of a ten-minute concrete demonstration (in which students role-played inviting different people to the same social event) to help make sense of a freewrite question in a new class one year later. The topic was "language variation."

> Our topic today proved to me that a concrete demonstration really does help you to remember something. When I took EDCI 320 a year ago Dr. Bayer did a demonstration on language variation and when we had to do a freewrite [on this topic] for this week, the first thing I thought of was "dialect" . . . I remembered the demonstration and an "Oh Yeah!" flashed in my head. Language variation is also the change in language according to social context. For example, you would talk differently to your close friend than to a professor. The words you choose would change and so would your tone of voice. In dialect variation the variables are pronunciation, grammar, vocabulary and morphology. Cognitive schemata (culture, prior knowledge and experience) and social context (audience, purpose) cause language variation. Again, audience and purpose is an important consideration.

FOCUSED READING

Having started with what the students know about a particular topic and guided students through appropriate scaffolding activities, the teachers asked their students to look for confirmation of their current thinking in the reading material.

Surprisingly few teachers reported problems with comprehension of texts. It may be that by the time students were engaged extensively in reading they had enough knowledge about the topic (and were *conscious* of that knowledge) to make connections with ideas in texts. Nonetheless, the teachers felt a few techniques for focusing reading showed some promise.

One workable technique was the Informal Prediction Guide shown on the opposite page in which students generated their own questions about what they thought would be in the text and then read for confirmation of their ideas.

The following excerpt reflects this perspective:

> These were more successful than the formal guides. First of all, students were able to generate questions that were of interest to THEM. Students may have seen the formal prediction guides as being too test-like and more difficult to understand [teacher's language]. Informal Prediction Guides are in their own language.

Prediction Guides

3 min.,   What do you think the film <u>Beyond Honolulu</u> is going
         to be about?

I think this film will talk about Hawaiia Coral reefs on the outer shores of Hawaii and may be about some of the native birds.

In regards to science, the film titled "Beyond Honolulu" will be about the animals surrounding the Hawaiian Islands and of the rest of the Pacific. It talks about the marine animals in the ocean.

Write three questions that you think will be answered in
the text.

How do they reproduce?
What do they eat?
Where do they live?
What is the bird's structure like?
What is a bird's habitat like?
What do birds eat?

Students can also brainstorm what they predict they will find in their readings and look for confirmation of their predictions as they read.

Once again the importance of modeling is illustrated by with how quickly students comprehend a new procedure:

> The Informal Prediction Guide went off on tangents. I tried to replicate the demonstration provided in the [college] class. First, to develop a few questions from the title of a reading, and then to read for confirmation. However, in my practicum, the students developed questions that were not related to the title of the article . . . I should have provided the students with a concrete experience of focused reading . . . before giving it to individual students. I probably moved too quickly letting students work alone before they had any prior knowledge or prior understanding of concept "focused reading."

I have found in my own teaching that the time it takes to model a new procedure or strategy that students are supposed to use is worth it and pays off in the long run.

Again, why spend time building prior knowledge and focusing reading before asking students to read their text? Because as one teacher reported "They seem to have better comprehension . . . . "

DISCOVERING AREAS OF STUDENT CONFUSION

There are several vehicles that can help students who have difficulty comprehending the text or class discussions. One of these vehicles is the problem-solving group, in which members help each other clarify and expand their thinking. As students gain experience working in collaborative small groups to accomplish meaningful tasks, group-related problems diminish, although they never disappear totally. Few teachers mentioned problems with using peer problem-solving groups. You can see why heterogeneous groups are so important. The more diverse the group membership, the more likely someone in the group has some prior knowledge on a given topic.

A second vehicle available to students who need some assistance is the think/write log. It takes modeling, practice, time, and an acceptance of the purpose for students to use these logs effectively. The first experiments with using think/write logs (also known as learning logs or journals) did lead to some unexpected results. Renee asked her elementary students to respond to the question "What do you want to know more about?" One student wrote, "I was wondering why God made things"—a wonderful question illustrating how logs can meet the needs of individual students.

How specific should the directions for logs be? I think it depends on their purpose. I ask my university students to use them (1) to make clear to themselves the connections they can make between new ideas discussed and read and their prior knowledge; (2) to ask me questions about areas of confusion; (3) to express their personal reactions to ideas; (4) to initiate questions that have not been brought up in class; and (5) to keep a record of questions they might like to investigate further in a long-term project.

I model think/write logs by showing examples of logs written by former students. I find that initial directions to university students need to include some kind of structure until they have had some practice with using writing in this manner. I ask my students to respond to the questions "What is unclear?" and "What do you want to know more about?"

The same questions can be used at any grade level, as they were in the following example.

> Kristy
>
> The English explorers were John Cabot, Sir Francis Drake and Sir Walter Raleigh. John Cabot found the Grand Bank, without meaning to and Sir Francis Drake was robbing Spanish galleons and was the second person to circumnavigate the world. Sir Walter Raleigh wanted to start a colony on Roanoke Island. But he failed because crops didn't grow well on the soil. Sir Walter Raleigh left some people on Roanoke Island but when he came back in 3 years they weren't there.
>
> What isn't clear to me is that how did the people that were left on Roanoke Island dissappear in 3 years?

But while these questions worked for this fifth grader, many elementary students found them too vague, at least in the beginning. Lori shares what happened in her seventh- and eighth-grade English classes:

> These (logs) did not work very well for the first 3-4 weeks . . . It appeared that the students did not take well to the terms *clear/unclear* so I changed the terminology of the logs. I revised it to "What I learned/understood" and "What I did not understand/questions." This way the students who had trouble previously found it easier to simply ask me a question. This proved to be successful. The first time I noticed the logs improving was a happy moment! Interesting questions were brought up and I addressed them at the next session. I found out that some students were still unclear about the fact that the Greek gods and goddesses we were studying were not real Greek human beings. This is something that might have gone unnoticed if it had not been brought to my attention through the logs. I also found that pulling student questions to be discussed and answered in class helped to model the types of questions one could ask in the logs.

Many teachers reported the problem of students not trusting the collaborative teacher-student relationship underlying this use of writing as a tool for learning. Elaine said of her high school students "In the first few logs, students wrote for the 'teacher as examiner.' They were very careful about their choice of words and worked very hard at writing the 'correct response'—what they thought I wanted."

Responding to the content only, not grading the logs, and engaging in a genuine dialogue with the student eventually seems to allay most anxieties. Teachers in the middle elementary grades seemed to have more success if they used the term *learning letters* rather than *think/write logs*.

> The think/write logs . . . proved a bit troublesome at first for the same reasons as the focused freewrite—the fear of being graded. With the think/write logs, there seemed to be a greater fear in the students because they had to demonstrate, via their entries, what they had just learned. Once again, they needed to be reassured that their think/write logs would not be graded.
>
> I felt that the students did not seem truly relaxed with the concept of the think/write logs. It was suggested by my support group members that I change the think/write logs to "learning letters," which really fit in with the mail system set up in my classroom. I have created mailboxes for both the students and the teacher. Up until this point we had utilized the mail system for our language arts sessions and simply for the pleasure of writing letters to one another. However, the concept and implementation of the learning letters proved wonderfully successful!!

Marilyn also notes that "Learning letters" instead of "Think/Write" logs worked well because the students looked forward to a personal written correspondence with the teacher.

This age student is quite familiar with letter writing; it makes sense that they would feel comfortable using what they already know about corresponding with others. Karen discovered this in her class:

> The think/write logs were successful . . . after I asked them to pretend that they were writing a letter to me . . . Before, the logs were not what I expected . . . Only until I sat and stared at my desk at all the scratch paper and cut-out hearts that said "I love you Mrs. Mukai" and "You are nice and I wish you could stay" did I realize that these students could pour their hearts out if done on a personal level. So, I asked them to "talk" to me. And it worked! I started to receive more information about what they learned, what was confusing, and what they did and did not like. It was exciting to discover areas of confusion and dislikes since such topics are rarely talked about in a "traditional" classroom. And it was especially refreshing to read that they enjoyed a certain lesson and actually learned something!

Marilyn and Karen's learning letter technique illustrates the adaptability of CAL. Teachers generated various strategies appropriate for their various teaching situations while remaining faithful to the collaborative-apprenticeship model.

In the early elementary (K–2) grades, teachers reported that their students also had some difficulty at first because they were inexperienced with using writing as a tool for learning; the students didn't realize that it was OK to use invented spelling to convey their thinking and feelings about what was going on in class. Sherry, Carol, Alison, and Sharyl, members of a novice teacher support group, collaborated on their proposed solutions:

What did we do?

1. A safe, secure atmosphere was established. For example, assuring students that they were not being graded.
2. Modeling as a class helped students to understand what they were supposed to do.
3. Making the question more explicit (change "What was clear?" to "What kinds of things does a doctor do?") helped students understand how to respond.
4. Through time, the students realized that they could take risks in a classroom.

Elaine, working with ESL students at the college level, says that:

With older students, as well as younger, specificity is helpful in directing think-write logs. However, a more important discovery is that think/write logs work. I found evidence of students using logs to prepare for tests, to summarize daily lessons, and to solve areas of confusion.

DECIDING WHAT
TO CORRECT

Sometimes my colleagues at the university level express concern about being placed in the role of grammarians; they don't have time to "correct" more papers. This same concern is expressed by content-area teachers at the secondary and elementary levels. The concern is legitimate. After participating in workshops, however, these instructors seem to become more comfortable with the idea that promoting student language competence within their disciplines is not a matter of "correcting" or "not correcting." Students can use expressive writing and talk while they are in the process of assimilating new ideas. Logs and problem-solving group talk need not be "corrected." They need responses to the content. When students explore tentatively held concepts in longer-term projects, they can also collaborate to help each other assimilate and develop their ideas. Peer writing groups, for example, can provide students with feedback leading to the necessary revision and editing for the transactional writing pieces or oral presentations required within various academic disciplines.

Not everything during this process needs to be graded either. Expressive writing in the form of freewrites, logs, and first drafts need responses to the students' messages. Sometimes instructors use "credit/no credit" for participation in these activities. For written pieces that will be turned in for evaluation, students can help each other through the arduous process of developing newly assimilated ideas to share one's interpretation, point of view, or conclusions about a particular issue. This collaboration includes helping prepare the final product by checking spelling, grammar, mechanics, and so on. The instructor can be useful during this process by holding short one-to-one student-teacher conferences or by responding directly to writing group requests.

CHANGED ATTITUDES

At all levels, teachers noticed a change in their attitudes when they experimented with using language as a tool for learning within content areas. Lois, a high school teacher, came to believe that

> The basic idea in writing, talking, and reading as tools for learning is that they are forms of communication which students feel comfortable to use with their teachers. These are nonthreatening techniques which promote questioning . . . which is so important in learning. This, in turn, creates an atmosphere of understanding and respect between teacher and student.

Karen began to think about helping students develop their reading and writing skills within content-area instruction.

> First, the content areas have become of great importance to me. I no longer regard them as "less academic" than reading and language arts. In fact, I plan to spend more time on them . . . and to teach the reading and language arts skills within those lessons.

Haunani connects the language processes and the content-areas:

> Prior to my learning experience [with CAL], I had a limited sense of how language could be used in the content area. Beyond the traditional comprehension question-and-answer sections at the end of textbook chapters and research reports, my knowledge of how to utilize language as a tool in content areas was very limited . . . I have now acquired a new schema for using language in a science classroom, and can apply this toward other content areas as well. I have come to feel that students must view their reading, writing, speaking, and listening as purposeful and meaningful and that there are a multitude of ways to implement these learning tools within any subject area.

CAL follows language and learning principles that are found in a number of classrooms today. The best-known at the elementary level are the whole language classrooms. While there is no single term used for implementation of these principles at the secondary and college levels, many of these teaching situations are associated with or influenced by the National Writing Project (NWP) or the writing across the curriculum (WAC) movement.

Students in these classrooms are viewed as active learners who use language as a tool for learning. Changing the role of the student and broadening the use of language usually dictates other changes as well. The rest of this chapter will focus on this "ripple effect."

ORGANIZING SCHEDULES AND CLASSROOMS

It takes time for students to work together in small groups and to write and revise writing pieces. While making changes of any kind is difficult I think the blocks of time already built into the elementary schedule offer real possibilities for change, as many educators who run whole language and other integrated programs already know. Blocks of time are usually built into the schedule for language arts and reading, and it is possible to consider using these blocks of time differently. For example, language development could be supported by using reading, writing, talking, and listening as tools for learning within the elementary content areas.

Doing so might decrease the two to three hours now set aside for language arts and reading instruction as we know it and increase the time scheduled for the content areas. It would not, however, eliminate time for students to "curl up" with a book of their own choosing or time to work on their various writing pieces both privately and in collaboration with others.

Secondary education schedules often follow a fifty-minute period, six-period-a-day schedule with teachers working with upwards of 150 students a day. Fifty minutes is a short period of time for the teacher and students to become engaged in talking, listening, reading, and writing about complex issues. How can you fit CAL into fifty-minute periods? Thinking through an overall plan for the introduction of a major concept would provide the teacher with some guidance for determining how much time it would take. For example, it might take fifty minutes to elicit and share prior knowledge and prepare students to look for confirmation of their knowledge in an upcoming scaffolding activity.

It may take one to three fifty-minute periods to introduce, work through, and connect student-generated information to the concept under study. Having used student involvement in this activity to focus their out-of-class reading, at the following session problem-solving groups might spend fifteen to twenty minutes collaborating to clarify areas of confusion.

As students assume more responsibility for their own learning and are involved in longer-term projects, more of each session would be scheduled for collaborative work in small groups as students increasingly use them as resources.

This tentative schedule for using CAL does not mean that the fifty-minute schedule is destiny. A number of secondary schools use some kind of rotating class schedule, such as an A day and a B day, which allows for longer class periods. Classes run eighty to ninety minutes, which increases the probability that the students will have time to become involved. These longer blocks of time also provide opportunities to integrate subject areas, such as literature and history.

Although higher education schedules often have short class periods like those of secondary schools, here, too, it is possible to consider longer sessions. I typically run my classes on a Tuesday, Thursday schedule, which gives me one hour and thirty minutes per session or one three-hour block. If learning is primarily social, learners need time to interact with each other.

PHYSICAL ARRANGEMENT

Form follows function. I think this can be seen clearly if we look at most of our classrooms, where desks are lined up in rows, and at our large theatre-like lecture halls. These physical arrangements reflect teaching-learning models in which the teacher is the transmitter of knowledge and the student is the passive recipient. If the functions of the classroom residents are modified and students become active learners engaged with each other and the instructor in using language as a tool for learning, how would the physical arrangements change?

Flexibility would play a key role. If students are going to be engaged in various collaborative tasks in which group membership changes frequently, a physical arrangement that allows movement without chaos would be helpful. I was quite fascinated when touring the new building at Harvard Medical School that was designed to reflect the new team approach Harvard has implemented in its medical education program called Pathways. There is only one lecture hall; all the other rooms are small classrooms or seminar rooms where team members can meet and work with each other and their professors. The professor's role is more often that of resource person than lecturer. The school has accommodated its physical arrangements to reflect a teaching-learning model that emphasizes collaboration. Of course not every school can build a building that reflects a shift in their teaching-learning paradigm, but it is possible to have movable chairs instead of desks nailed to the floor.

We do not live or work in a vacuum, so it comes as no surprise that changing teaching-learning models also affects how teachers see themselves in relation to students, how students' self-perceptions change, how both view the curriculum, and how articulation occurs with those outside the classroom. These are the subjects of the final chapter.

7

CHANGING
TEACHING
MODELS

CHANGING ROLES:
TEACHERS AND STUDENTS

The solutions to problems that the experienced and novice teachers developed reflect the view that as professionals they have both the responsibility and the competence to make decisions on their own. This perspective of teacher as decision maker is compatible with the terms *teacher as learner* and *teacher as collaborator;* they all reflect the concept of professional educators as continually modifying their teaching strategies according to new knowledge, personal experiences, and feedback from students. Students are seen as active learners involved in trying to make sense out of school-related tasks. As active learners they take increasing responsibility for directing their own learning, and they are capable of providing instructors with feedback.

This view of teaching-learning represents a different model from the one I experienced as a student and tried to emulate in the early part of my teaching career. That model described a teacher as a transmitter of knowledge and students as passive recipients. Over the years I've made the decision to move away from teacher as transmitter and toward teacher as collaborator to try to remain consistent with current language and learning principles.

How do other teachers in transition view their own change? In the following excerpts we catch glimpses of instructors redefining the teacher-student relationship as they experiment with the collaborative-apprenticeship learning model. Sandi, for example, writes:

I have modified my teaching practices. My previous idea of a science lesson was lecture-reading-comprehension questions-test. My schemata now utilizes freewriting, scaffolding activities, focused reading, think/write logs, student talk and application activities. I attempt to take the students into consideration when planning lessons and attempt to make their learning more enjoyable and meaningful.

Undoubtedly, my belief of the role of a teacher has changed drastically. I no longer see myself as "controller" or "dictator." I am now a support system, allowing my students to be active, independent learners rather than passive, dependent students. Scaffolding is now part of my vocabulary.

I also view the students in a different light. The students can be teachers too. I learned this from my third grader, Michael. Peer interaction facilitates learning. Students have knowledge that can be shared with the class. Student talk does not mean wasting time.

Sandi will write more about Michael later in the chapter.

"Letting go," or sharing control, is an issue that Linda thinks about.

The role of teacher has changed for me too. Rather than always giving out information and controlling the learning, I found it is much more effective to allow the students to interact and have more control of their learning. They become active participants in learning.

As these teachers talk about how they see themselves changing as teachers, they, like Karen below, invariably mention the changing role of the student.

The [CAL] Framework has changed my ideas of the role of the teacher. I have always felt that the role of the teacher should be facilitative and yet functional. But, after reaching the classroom and being bombarded with tons of work and academic problems, I found it hard to be anything but an authoritarian! Somehow, it "took care" of the discipline problems . . . but only temporarily, not permanently. The Framework has forced me to step back and evaluate my reasons for becoming a teacher. I seemed to have lost them when the parental pressures of a private school began to take control of my better judgment. By . . . using . . . focused freewrites and brainstorming, I have allowed the students to tell me what they know or want to know. I have given them the chance to defend their roles as students! My role of the teacher has turned facilitative in nature . . . I have learned to respect my profession and appreciate myself as well as the children.

All of the instructors in this book, including myself, are in transition; we are each somewhere along a continuum with teacher as transmitter on one end and teacher as collaborator on the other end. Most of us are moving toward teacher as collaborator because we believe it to be a more effective teaching-learning model. Roman suggests that this model may also help with teacher burnout:

Before . . . I was wondering about the teaching methods I would use. I wanted to get away from the lecture method as much as possible: I've felt for a long time that it is not that important for the student to master what the teacher thinks and then regurgitate it back to him, but rather, it is important for the student to develop his own critical thinking capacities and to form his own point of view.

One of the particular things that I like is the looking at students as collaborators in the educational process. They start as novices . . . , but as the learning process goes along the students gain in ability and confidence and soon they are capable of teaching the teacher as well. . . . I also think that the active interchange between the students themselves as well as between the students and the teacher would help to keep the teacher involved in the discipline and not get tired of teaching the same material year after year after year. Perhaps this makes teacher burnout less likely?

But change is scary. Anna offers words of encouragement.

The first step should simply be to try it. Even if you just take one step—elicit students' prior knowledge on a subject matter—that really helps. You'll see a difference in their motivation and interest. This is what will get you trying more and more and is the greatest reward for the teacher.

And Jean, who has eighteen years' teaching experience and is now a beginning teachers' supervisor for grades K–12, has found that

Given this basic teaching-learning model, planning, making instructional decisions, and evaluating become easier and more systematic for the novice teacher. With a wide range of students to face each day, this language-based instruction honors students for their individuality and fosters success in each. Teachers are not dealing with the development of separate lessons for each student yet achieve the goals of individualized instruction and student ownership of learning.

As teachers become more confident in the use of the model, a shift in their teaching occurs, from the use of structured materials and lesson plans to the students as determiners for planning and instruction. As teachers gain success in the teaching-learning process, not only is hesitancy overcome, but a true integration of the model occurs as teachers view themselves as learners.

What about the students' reactions to these changing roles? The previous chapter on problems and solutions highlighted students' hesitancy about change. Students arrive in classes with highly structured "world views" of the classroom based on their own experiences. Most of them have been on the receiving end of the teacher as transmitter model; they know they are to receive information from the instructor and give it back in tests, reports, or question-and-answer sessions. Collaborating with one's peers has not been encouraged, and the teacher has always done most of the talking. Whoa!! All of a sudden the instructor is asking them to write their goals for this class or to share with their peers what they already know about a subject. As the teachers noted in Chapter 6, it took some time, practice, modeling, and a sense that somehow these changes made sense to diminish the students' hesitancy.

A particularly interesting phenomenon occurs when students are viewed as collaborators within a classroom setting; the "student expert" emerges. This becomes more obvious in my classroom from the middle to the end of the semester, when my students are engaged in long-term projects involving self-selected topics. They investigate particular areas of interest to them within the discipline in which we are involved, and they often come up with points of view, make connections, discover a piece of information that we haven't thought about before. But this student expert role also comes up much earlier in the semester, sometimes from the very first day of class when students share what they already know about the topic. Sometimes some of the students are more expert than the teacher about issues that come up in class. Sandi Wong shares her experience of the student expert role within a third-grade science students who were primarily from the Philippines or Samoa.

> At times, students had more prior knowledge and concrete experiences than I did. For example, in my third-grade class, Michael shared his fish stories with the class. Since Michael's family went fishing every weekend, Michael had a lot of information on fishing. . . . Obviously, Michael was more of an expert on this subject than I was. So, I stepped aside and let Michael lead the discussion. The students were thrilled with the stories and were captivated with Michael's experiences. Michael's presentation was much more interesting and held greater credibility than mine. I suppose the reason why Michael's talk worked out so well was because Michael . . . was able to speak at their level and in a manner that was easily understood by the class. Hence, students learned from each.
>
> I am just beginning to tap into the vast reservoir of student knowledge and experiences. Since I do have students from Samoa and the Philippines, their backgrounds are different from mine. I could learn from them too.

Sandi also comments on her students' reactions to taking more responsibility for their own learning.

> I also enjoyed the idea of scaffolding. Being a new teacher, I always make the mistake that as a teacher, I control everything. Scaffolding allows the teacher to be a supporter not the dictator. The teacher supports the students by filling in the gaps of knowledge . . . until the students can work independently. This worked in my class because I found that students prefer to be independent. . . .

Through student responses in think/write logs Sandi also found that her students were willing to take the initiative to seek clarification and go beyond minimum requirements.

> The greatest of my achievements was the think/write logs. . . . By reading their entries, I could tell that the students were reading for comprehension.

Previously, they were not bothered if they didn't understand the reading. Now, if parts are unclear, the students would reread the passage or ask me to clarify it for them. Sometimes, students would ask for more information about a subject . . . they volunteered to research the topic further.

I was surprised how well the think/write logs worked. The students retained more information by writing in their logs than they did by answering comprehension questions. I suppose that since the students were given a choice and could select portions which were important to them rather than what was important to the teacher, the learning became more meaningful.

Making learning more meaningful includes an examination of not only how we teach but also What and Why—the topic of the following section.

CHANGING THE CURRICULUM

Many of the teachers in transition we have heard from began to change by focusing on their teaching strategies but continuing to use the content and structure of the traditional curriculum. It is difficult enough to reconceptualize the teaching-learning relationship without having to worry about whether the curriculum content needs to be changed. Of course this issue has to be addressed eventually. It becomes clear to teachers in pursuit of broad conceptual goals that the traditional curriculum is sometimes too fragmented or too superficial in its presentation of interesting and complex issues.

Most of the teachers quoted in this book work within an embedded tradition called "covering the curriculum." This notion is connected to the view of a teacher (especially in K–12 grades) as a technician or manager who carries out lesson plans written by someone else, usually the authors of teachers' manuals. Teachers are instructed to work their way through the program or textbook. This covering-the-curriculum perspective is deeply embedded in our educational traditions. It shows up early in the teachers'-in-training think/write logs and in college class discussions. A typical log entry follows:

In Chapter 5 they talk about teachers who feel they have to cover so many chapters in the text so the students are prepared for the next year. The problem I have is we just don't have enough time in the school year to cover American History, for example. Every year we only get to the "Civil War Era" and still there is so much "good stuff" we haven't covered. Now whether they "learn" it or not is another story, along with whether they really need it or not.

In excerpts from his think/write log Stan shares his discovery that covering the curriculum leads to the memorization of facts but not necessarily the understanding of major concepts.

We [teachers at his elementary school] had a . . . discussion last week
. . . As we talked we never really spoke of "concepts"; it was more facts we
wanted them to learn. We discussed this at the end but I left feeling that we
are missing the point in some ways because we as teachers don't know the
concepts we are supposed to be teaching them. In the articles I have been
reading . . . one of the problems we have in education is that teachers don't
know the concepts or understand them enough to teach them.

I find myself teaching the students the facts on the southeast region,
which we are about to finish, but lately I have been asking myself, aren't
there some concepts that I should be trying to get them to learn and
understand? They know the states, capitols, major rivers and lakes, land
forms and economic activities but is that all they need to know? What
concepts should go along with geography like this? Are they written and
do we have to find them or are we as teachers supposed to develop our own
depending upon our own decisions we have made about our students and
their needs? It is another area where I feel I have a lack of thorough
understanding.

Covering the curriculum can mean "covering the facts" if the facts are not
related to a broad conceptual framework underlying a particular content
area. Stan raises reasonable questions about curriculum in his personal
examination of what and why.

If students are going to develop as competent thinkers and language
users, they need to be engaged on a regular basis with complex problem-
solving tasks—meaningful tasks in which facts are related to concepts.
This is Stan's goal. The next two excerpts reflect his thinking as he works
toward it.

We talked about concepts at this meeting and for awhile I felt like I was
learning more about specific info that kids learn. But the more I think about
it, I'm beginning to see some concepts come out of my region units. One
could be major cities are almost always on the coast or a major river or lake.
Another is latitude will determine your culture.

The students are beginning to make predictions about economic activities, natural resources and climate that they didn't have a clue about when
this unit began.

In his last log Stan writes:

I feel like I made a big step in my social studies region and the search for
concepts. We are starting to see that two things have influenced the
development of cities, states and our style of living. They are water and
climate. All major cities are near lakes, rivers or oceans. I'm trying to help
the kids see this, which they do, and be able to explain why.

The climate also influences our lives, our homes, our clothes and our life
styles. The climate varies all over the country but the extreme difference is
winter and it is colder and more extreme as the latitude gets higher.

In reading my learning logs now, I am trying to see not only if they know
the specifics of each region, but also how all regions are similar and differ-

ent and *why*. I can see how these concepts can be developed over a period of time.

Teachers such as Stan have come to see themselves as teacher-learners capable of critical examination of curriculum.

What are the consequences of not covering the curriculum? Roman, who is preparing to teach high school history, raises this question, which comes up over and over in discussions with instructors considering change. He wants to know how you can teach the same amount of content if you are going to take class time to allow peers to work with each other in various small groups:

> Did this teaching method limit the amount of material that could be covered? It is obvious to me that the material studied and absorbed by using writing, peer group discussions, and so on will be well-absorbed and well-learned. The question I had was not one of quality, but rather quantity. For example, could a teacher of biology teach an entire standard biology textbook using this method? Or could a teacher of social studies cover and have the students learn the content of an American history textbook that covered pre-Columbus America to the present?

Roman chose the latter topic for his I-Search paper. In his readings, he came across Toby Fulwiler's (1987) work, *Teaching with Writing*, and found an answer that satisfied him.

> I think that Toby Fulwiler (1987) in one of his latest works, *Teaching with Writing*, comes as close as anyone to answering this question concerning the amount of content that can be taught when using the "Reading and Writing Across the Disciplines" approach . . . "you won't have as much time yourself to disseminate information and cover material; for the group process to work well, the groups will need class time both to plan and present. But consider that the loss in the sheer amount of information which can be covered will be more than offset by the learner responsibility and, consequently, by the depth of questioning and strength of retention" (142–143).

Connected to this difficult issue of covering the curriculum is the lack of integration between and within various curriculum areas. Math is typically taught separately from science; literature is divorced from history. Language instruction is often taught with a minimum of content. For example, writing instruction is separate from reading instruction and is likely to be further fragmented into isolated textbook lessons on grammar, spelling, and mechanics. Students have to make sense of this fragmented curriculum, but it is difficult to do. They are hard-pressed to make connections between the activities in which they are engaged throughout the school day.

Much of the work of whole language teacher-scholars has been in trying to remedy this problem of fragmentation. Various descriptions of integrated curriculums can be found in the whole language literature, particularly at the elementary level.

How can educators begin the process of examining curriculum? It is no easy task to reach agreement on the what and why? of the curriculum at a particular school. Having established some sense of the "big picture," teachers then have to think about where integration would be appropriate. An individual teacher will not always want to seek the big picture alone. Working with one's peers and administrators in on-site study groups (Bayer 1985) is one of the least expensive, easiest to implement, and most effective ways to bring about resolutions regarding change. Volunteers from various grade levels across content areas meet on a regular basis (perhaps monthly) to examine current teaching practices and curriculum, read and attend workshops, record and share what's happening in their own classrooms, argue about possible resolutions that would improve current status, try out decisions in their own classrooms, and share their conclusions with the faculty at large. In such an ongoing staff development program teachers themselves are participants in the collaborative learning process.

I emphasize on-site decision-making because this idea is compatible with current movements supporting increased autonomy for the classroom teacher to make professional decisions in collaboration with peers and the administration.

CHANGING TEACHER PLANNING

Suppose the instructor is viewed as a professional capable of making curriculum decisions that facilitate language development and complex thinking. Suppose further that students are viewed as active learners who need to be involved in tasks they see as meaningful and meeting their intentions. What does planning look like for these classrooms? Planning involves some view of the big picture (or conflicting big pictures) within a particular content area. As Stan discovered, the instructor needs to (1) be conscious of the major concepts within a course of study, and (2) acknowledge that the concepts are likely to be expanded or modified by students' interests and insights. In other words, long-term planning is likely to occur! Instead of covering the curriculum indiscriminately, teachers will make choices that best support the conceptual framework.

What I do at the university level is sit down in July or August and sketch out in expressive writing what I think are the major concepts within a particular course that I will be teaching the following semester. I typically end up with five or six concepts that build on each other. For example, for the course described in this book, I thought it was important to consider current literature on how individuals learn, how individuals learn language, how language is used as a tool for learning, and what the implications are for using all the language processes (writing, reading, talking, listening) for learning in our classrooms.

I use that broad sequence as a guide for choosing texts and journal articles. I then think of how I can start from the students' frames of reference regarding these concepts and how I can help them expand their background knowledge. As you well know the process that I use is reflected in the CAL framework. Long-term planning helps me be at ease with the idea that the direction of the course will be modified by student interests, student initiative, and student feedback and that students will assume increasing responsibility for their learning.

Below one teacher in transition shares how she has changed her planning to be consistent with her changing teaching-learning strategies.

> My plans for the week or the semester have differed since my adoption of the learning framework. I first review the Unit, the chapter titles and content, and decide on the major concepts or objectives I want my students to grasp about the Unit. My next decision is how I will use each chapter to contribute to the Unit objectives. These decisions help me to be more selective of the material I focus on in each chapter. I am less overwhelmed by the quantity of material to be covered because of the quality of content I choose to develop in depth. . . . In introducing new Units or chapter . . . [students] write . . . predictions about what the chapters may contribute to the concepts of the Unit. Each lesson planned thereafter includes scaffolding activities which [uses] students' prior knowledge of the concept to be developed.
>
> Teacher planning involves more than day-to-day assignments in a textbook. It involves my seeing the overall picture. . . . Worksheets are not that necessary in my instructional plan, but meaningful, purposeful writing and collaboration are. Guiding students to set purposes for reading and revealing ways to understand text are also important.

CHANGING EVALUATION

What issues come up about evaluating learning within the CAL model? The issues vary depending on the context within which you are working. When I was working in the middle school reading program, we gave no letter grades at all. Instead we wrote descriptions of what books the student was reading, had student and parent conferences, and conducted individual miscue reading inventories for some students.

At the university I initially followed the traditional practice of giving a midterm and a final examination to determine student competency. I found I needed to modify and expand on this procedure. Since my students are involved in peer groups a lot of the time, use expressive writing regularly, revise drafts, conduct panel discussions on particular issues, and work in practicum support groups, it didn't seem reasonable to evaluate their learning solely on the use of exams, even if they were essay exams. So I added a "credit/no credit" component. I minimized exams and had students submit final written products on self-selected topics for letter grade evaluation.

I give credit/no credit for activities that are course requirements because they require student participation such as taking part in peer problem-solving and writing groups, focused freewriting, and keeping think/write logs. If students turn in their think/write logs, for example, they get a "credit"; if they don't, they get a "no credit." Students are using language as a tool for learning course concepts. These ongoing activities reflect apprentice attempts to assimilate ideas; later they may reflect attempts to

Pre-teaching activity: 3 min. focused free writing.

F ish

Fish

There are two kinds of fish fresh water fish and salt water fish. Most of the fresh water fish live in streams, ponds, lakes, etc. Salt water fish live in the sea. all fish have fins.

A fishes tail may depend on how fast it swims a fish with a bold tail swims faster than a fish with a smaller tail challenge ideas. Feeling free to take risks, ask questions, propose hypotheses, and admit confusion is absolutely necessary for the apprentice learner. Grading these activities is likely to short-circuit the exploration of ideas. It is possible, however, to assess student development when sitting in on small group discussions and when reading student logs by noting both the connections students are making between ideas discussed in class and their own knowledge and how these connections develop over time. For example, the logs illustrated here come from a student in an elementary science course. The log shown on page 120 is from the focused freewriting activity used to elicit student knowledge about fish; the log below is from this student's think/write log entry indicating new knowledge.

Post-teaching activity: 3 min.   Think-write Log.
                           What is clear about fish?

Fish

There are two kinds of fish. Fishes made of cartilage and fishes made of bones. The fishes fins help them to manuver about in the water.

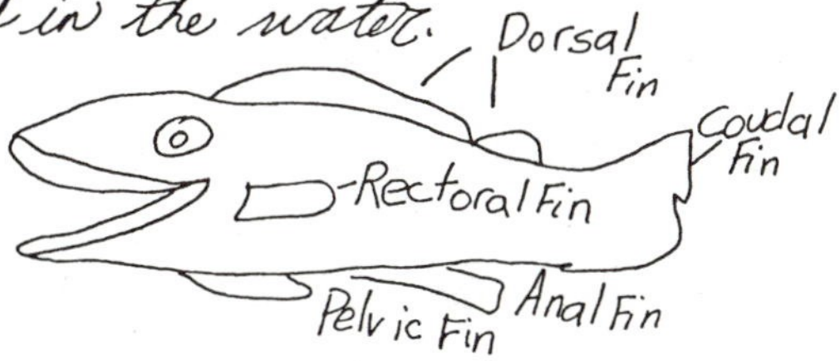

Dorsal Fin
Caudal Fin
Rectoral Fin
Pelvic Fin
Anal Fin

Some examples of fishes with bones are tuna, herring, salmon etc. They are an important source of food to people that live in Japan and other people that live along the coast. They are also used as fertilizer, and for pet food. One example of the fish made of cartillage is the shark. It is carnivous and swims constantly.

The next example comes from a high school English class. The student teacher, Tony Lee, was preparing his students for an introduction to Korean literature. First he wanted to know what they already knew about the country. Responding to the focused freewriting question "What comes to mind when I mention the word *Korea*?" this tenth grader made a list and then expanded on his ideas using the very informal prose characteristic of expressive writing (see the example below).

Tony discovered that his students generally knew very little about Korea and had great difficulty making sense of Korean literature. He backed away from the literature temporarily to provide scaffolding activities to help his students understand the political and social climate in which the literature was produced. Then his students returned to the literature. The resulting development can be seen in an excerpt from the same student's think/write log on the following pages.

Korea
1. Mash
2. War
3. people with black hair
4. short people
5. hot food
6. My uncle who went their during the Korean war.
7. Thats about all.

I don't know too much about Korea except from what I see on T.V. and from what I remember my uncle telling me. Both have to do with the war. You see, on T.V. I love to watch Mash and my uncle went to fight there. So I guess my only image of Korea has to do with fighting and death although Alan Alda is extemely funny.

My understanding has changed a lot. I feel I can understand it a whole lot more. Even the short stories are understandable. This is not to say I like Korean literature because I don't, but I can say it's not as foriegn to me anymore.

~~For~~ There are TWO things you kept on stressing: Universal and Regional themes and concepts. Metaphor is what's universal and Regional is ~~cultural~~ cultural factors. For Korea, whats thematic for them is a sense of fatalism due to the countries political ~~a~~ circumstance.

So when I look at this poem again I can see the use of metaphor. He is comparing the farm fields to and ~~an unborn~~ unborn child. The fields have been taken over and the farmers have nothing to look foward to. They have no hope. The unborn child symbolizes no future and no tomorrow. That's a Korean theme because it's fatalistic korean psychology is real depressing and out of it. The people are not united and families are constantly being separated.

> Most of the literature reflects that.
> Hey, I'm pretty proud of myself but
> I'll probably forget all of this next
> year. Maybe I won't.
> Anyways, like I said, I really don't
> care too much about Korean Literature because
> its too depressing for me. But I do
> understand that thats what the country
> is sort of like and so thats what
> the literature will reflect.

The second log excerpt reflects student assimilation of new ideas. Over the course of a school year logs document student language and thinking development, often more effectively than exams.

Teachers in transition found that students' grades typically went up. Alan, a high school student teacher, reports on what he and his supervising teacher discovered:

> I believe the use of the think-write logs and small group discussions were beneficial to the students and the teacher. The students were able to see the learning process in action by being given the opportunity to express their ideas more frequently than in the regular classroom. I think the fact that the teacher encourages students through his/her responses through the think/ write logs is another plus. It gives the students a different attitude toward school; everyone can learn . . . Finally, a note on evaluation. After we gave the lesson on intelligence and the brain, we gave the students a test and the scores were much improved over the averages of the previous test (done with just lecture and textbook), so we were pleased with the results.

COMMUNICATING CHANGE: ADMINISTRATORS AND PARENTS

The social origins of learning concept is not limited to our students' learning; it applies to all individuals. The term *teacher as learner* is now a familiar one in current literature, and one that suggests professional educators who view themselves as active learners willing to modify teaching practices according to new knowledge. Examples of staff development programs that are theoretically consistent with the social origins of learning concept include the highly regarded National Writing Project Summer Institutes, TAWL (whole language) Groups, and on-site study groups. These programs view teachers as active learners and promote collaborative activities in which teachers can share their various levels of expertise with each other.

Similar staff development programs are also available for administrators. *Administrators as learners* are administrators who view themselves as professional educators willing to modify administrative practices according to new knowledge. One example of this type of staff development program comes from a National Writing Project summer institute that Kathleen Andrasick and I directed in Hawaii. The group consisted of six elementary school principals, six high school principals, one state staff member, and two staff members from the school district's art and drama programs.

We engaged these participants in collaborative activities in which they wrote, talked, read, and listened to ideas about promoting student writing development across the curriculum (K–12). They experienced for themselves what was being suggested for the students at their respective schools. This group became so cohesive that they formed their own study group to continue the collaboration during the school year. A number of these principals were writing working papers on how to promote collaboration between administration and the teaching staff. I suspect that the faculty of such administrators as learners will feel comfortable approaching these principals with issues of change.

But one of the greatest worries of both the novice and the experienced teacher in transition is being evaluated harshly by an administrator for not running "a quiet classroom." Collaboration implies talk. Marilyn's remarks acknowledge the importance of supportive administrators.

> My class has always had a great deal of positive peer interaction. It is an integral part of the language arts program and so it easily transferred to content area instruction. It's good to know from reading the research and from the feedback in my support groups, however, that most other children also learn better when interacting with peers. I'm afraid I was guilty of the "quiet class" syndrome when I began my teaching career. I think for new teachers, especially, they feel it's risky to give the students so much control over their learning, and "noise," even productive noise, is a sign to many administrators that the teacher is lax on discipline. I'm lucky to be working at a school that is so enlightened!

If administrators are not familiar with the theoretical principles that support alternative teaching-learning models such as CAL, they may find it interesting to attend a National Writing Project summer institute, take a language across the curriculum course, or work with faculty to set up volunteer study groups to examine the pros and cons of such alternative models.

Principals have to be concerned about how to support change based on current theory and practice while reassuring parents. In my personal experience with the middle school reading program (which we changed from homogeneous ability grouping, in which students filled out skills workbooks, to a heterogeneously grouped program emphasizing self-selected reading material) we made packets for the parents. The packets included three handouts: one page of rationale supporting the changes; one page on how we were going to document student progress; and one page of references that parents could read to learn more about our approach. Our students also put together and conducted a slide show for Parents' Night explaining how and why they spent their class time as they did.

Our principal supported us all the way. Within a year parental concerns began to diminish as they became familiar with why we were doing what we were doing and, more importantly, noticed that their children were reading more.

Parents have developed their own view of education from their own experiences as students. The only role model they have had may be the teacher as transmitter and student as passive learner. So it is only natural that an alternative teaching-learning model will cause anxiety until they understand that it is likely to facilitate the language and thinking competencies of their children.

Anna describes the reactions of colleagues, administrators, and parents to their classrooms, which do not look like the traditional classroom.

> Administrators and colleagues see a greater integration of Language Arts and content areas linked together and are quite pleased by it.
>
> Parents often wonder why worksheets aren't brought home by the children. However, when they see projects being displayed, brought home or presented for parent shows, they are very complimentary about what is being done in the classroom.

But what criteria would an administrator or peer (involved in peer evaluation) use to evaluate what is going on in classrooms using CAL? Jean, supervisor for beginning teachers K–12, shares her views on this issue.

> . . . I note the amount of student language use in the classroom, and how the teacher responds to the language activities and interaction among the students. Writing and talking become key indicators of a highly visible language based classroom.
>
> I also observe the effect of this teaching-learning process upon the students . . . their responsiveness . . . more on-task . . . engaged student behaviors . . . and increased learning and retention.
>
> . . . I look for connections to previous activities . . . and for how students are using their prior knowledge . . .
>
> . . . I look for evidence of students taking ownership of their own learning . . .

Students are listening, speaking, interacting with each other rather than working individually on worksheets and workbooks. While active, engaged students become the focus of the classroom, texts and instructional materials are provided as a resource to students. The instructional materials are not limited to commercial readers, but real reading material such as library books ... students are reading different kinds of materials, materials of their choice and interest.

These classrooms are not always buzzing with student talk of course; there are times when quiet is important for reading and listening purposes. The use of language depends on what is appropriate for the particular tasks in which the students are engaged.

CHANGING TEACHER EDUCATION

I see two major directions for the study of teacher education reform. One set of studies focuses on whether colleges of education should become graduate professional schools. Students would receive an undergraduate degree in another area and enter a college of education for a graduate program that would include a year-long internship or apprenticeship under the guidance of a master teacher.

The second group of studies is concerned with what is happening inside teacher education classrooms. The CAL model, for example, was shaped in part by an ongoing analysis of videotapes that documented the teacher-student and student-student interactions throughout a two-semester course.

Whatever reforms are considered, I think they have to be theoretically consistent with current knowledge about language and learning principles. These principles will be modified as we continue to learn, and the teaching-learning processes that we choose must remain up to date.

CONCLUSION

I started this book by saying that the CAL model evolved as a result of my attempts to synthesize what I found to be theoretically consistent, but often fragmented, pieces of a teaching-learning model. I wanted a model that reflected a change in teacher-student relationships, clarified the ways the various language processes facilitated learning, and promoted interaction among peers.

The CAL model is not a linear, lockstep teaching method, but a guide for novices and experienced teachers in transition. It is a framework that reflects "work in progress," not a finished building. Indeed, when working with CAL you will discover strategies that work better than those included in this book. Those of you working in different grade levels and content areas will be able to refine, clarify, and explain your adaptations. I hope you will share.

APPENDIX 1

PRACTICUM INFORMATION

PRACTICUM SUPPORT GROUPS

In addition to short-term problem-solving groups and ongoing peer writing response groups, each class member belongs to a practicum support group. Because I teach at a college of education, it is not enough that my students assimilate course concepts; they have to gain experience with implementing these concepts in the elementary and secondary schools. They have to analyze the degree to which particular ideas seem to facilitate or hinder their students' learning.

We use the following practicum format:

Practicum

Option A: Five-week practicum in a content-area
 class: Three times a week/one-hour sessions

Option B: Seven-week practicum in a content-area
 class: Twice a week/one-hour sessions

If you are currently teaching content-area subjects, I encourage you to use your own class for this practicum and to consider inviting one or two of your colleagues who are not now teaching to work with you to plan and carry out this task. One major benefit for the experienced teacher in this arrangement is that you will have the opportunity to work alone with a small group of students.

Requirements: Implement the CAL model.

- Meet twice (or three times) a week with a content-area class for one hour each session (*minimum* requirement).
- Use the CAL model as your guide.
- Begin by *modeling* the concept of *freewriting* to elicit student knowledge when introducing a new concept.
- Preschool and kindergarten students can use *talk*.
- Provide scaffolding activities to help students expand their prior knowledge of topic *x*.
- Focus student reading with prediction guide techniques.
- Allow students to collaborate with each other in small groups so they can help each other assimilate the concepts being discussed.
- Introduce think/write logs toward the end of the unit.
- *Ask specific questions* of your students. (High school students may need to receive *credit* for this activity.)
- Model/demonstrate/discuss each new procedure beforehand.
- Share how *you* use these procedures. Keep a record of what worked, what didn't, and your thoughts on why or why not. *Ask your students these same questions.* Use this record as a basis for writing your Practicum Summary Paper. *Include examples of student work that illustrate your point.*
- *After the practicum* decide what you want to share about your practicum experiences with other support groups working in the same grade level or content area.

This particular course usually has about half the class currently teaching full-time, and half who are full-time college students. I do try to encourage the full-time teachers to invite class colleagues into their classrooms to carry out collaborative field experiences. Ultimately the college students must decide where (content area, grade level, school, collaborative or individual, etc.) to do the practicum. All participants then form practicum support groups (five or six per group) made up of individuals who are working in the same content area or grade level. Membership is flexible and pretty much determined by the students.

Group members begin the process of collaborating with each other to provide the support needed for successful practicum experiences. I provide class time for the groups to meet. At first I structure the group meetings by asking group members to come to the support group with "one successful strategy, procedure, etc. that they can share and one major problem they are having." Groups are essentially pooling their knowledge and calling on me to help them fill in gaps. As might be expected there are lots of problems in the beginning of the practicum. In many cases the students are working with tentative hypotheses about teaching-learning processes. There are doubts, and often support group members can help best. As Sharon says,

. . . I found I really needed to be flexible with my lessons, my attitude, and my beliefs. . . . when I first began the practicum, I was not really keen on the project because I felt a bit uncertain about the process . . . I discussed my feelings with my support group and found we were experiencing similar feelings, which really proved gratifying because we could discuss our ideas and truly brainstorm together. We offered suggestions and provided comfort, which allowed me to begin experimenting with the practicum. If a particular lesson or activity did not work, I learned to be flexible and evaluate what I had done. I could begin over, change my line of questioning . . . I believe the best activities relating to the framework in class were our meetings with the support groups and writing groups . . . we could help implement the very aspects of the framework in our practicum which we found to be successful for us as college students . . . To go through the process ourselves, we have a better understanding for what we need to establish as teachers in the content-areas.

Another student agrees:

I had never really appreciated peer interaction [but] I found the students especially helpful. I enjoyed sharing ideas about my practicum with my peers and I found their ideas and tips useful. It was great to find out that I was not the only one having problems. I especially liked the writing groups. This is the first time I have ever felt like I was in a community of learners. Like the high school students mentioned in one of the reports, I usually had relied on the professor's ideas rather than my peers. I realize that when the teacher makes the students see themselves as knowledgeable, then they perform accordingly.

In addition to collaborative projects, each student is responsible for analyzing his or her individual effort. Students keep logs like the following after each practicum session. I do not grade these logs; they help students develop the habit of analyzing the why as well as the what and the how of the educational choices they made.

ELEMENTARY SCIENCE CURRICULUM:

PRACTICUM LOG

Session 1 - 2/22/88

What Worked	What Didn't Work
1. Students meeting in small groups of 3–4 to discuss similarities and differences among group members about the FFW on "What is blood made of?"	1. Eliciting prior knowledge by doing a focused freewrite.

2. Students sharing with the rest of the class their group's similarities and differences while teacher verbally summarized.

How Do You Know It Worked?

1. As I walked around the room, students were sharing their FFW and exchanging ideas—some even debated about blood's composition.
2. Each group voluntarily shared their group's similarities and differences.

Why Do You Think It Worked?

1. People enjoy sharing what they have written to an audience which is familiar. People also like to share *their* past experiences with others.
2. Once again, sharing without feeling inferior because audience is familiar, allows students to freely share what they have discovered.

How Do You Know It Didn't?

1. Students didn't begin to write right away. I had to give many questions and examples before they could write. Students commented, "I don't know what to write—I don't know anything about blood."

Why Do You Think It Didn't?

1. I didn't model the process long enough for students to understand and carry out. I need to model the process until students feel comfortable and confident about doing the process on their own.

Student analysis seemed to help students reflect on their teaching and see patterns develop over a period of time. They discovered the value of long-term planning. Students also were not afraid to make their feelings known in these logs.

> To briefly summarize my comments on the practicum, I have three areas to discuss. The first comment is a complaint. Since I have to record each student's daily progress, I found writing a practicum log after every class very time consuming. Ten practicum logs might suffice.
> The second comment is a suggestion. I felt like I wanted to add "How to Improve" to the "What didn't work" column. This would allow me an opportunity to redeem myself from my depth of failure. I did take the liberty to add this to . . . one of my log entries.
> The third comment is confession. My biggest flaw in my teaching was being egocentric, viewing the world from my eyes. I used to assess the success of my lessons by my opinions only. After filling out 14 logs, I have learned to observe students' behavior and students' assignments. The column "How do you know it worked?" was the catalyst to my new sense of awareness. I am learning to view teaching from the students' point of view and not only my own.

APPENDIX 2

SAMPLE PRACTICUM
LESSON PLANS

A COLLABORATIVE-APPRENTICESHIP PROCESS FRAMEWORK

(Science—Kindergarten Level)

Teaching-Learning Cycle	Sample C.A.L. Framework in a Content Area	Students Using *Language* to Learn
	Session 1	
Select major concept.	*Concept*	*Students talk* about what they know.
	Animals in the sea protect themselves in many different ways.	
Start with what students know about concept using brainstorming or "think-pair-share" procedure.	*Vocabulary*	
	protection posion	
	defense electricity	
Make public what students know. Use small groups so students can pool their knowledge; small groups share knowledge with whole class. Collective prior knowledge becomes accessible to instructor and to others.	*"Background Group Discussion* Think-pair-share" procedure. Given the question, "What are some of the different ways animals in the sea protect themselves?" children think independently for 1–2 minutes, then find a partner and share what they know for 3–5 minutes. Teacher models and facilitates the sharing of knowledge as she floats among the pairs. Children and teacher then form the large group again and share what they talked about and learned.	*Students collaborate* with each other using *exploratory talk*.
		Students look for confirmation of their current knowledge in scaffolding activities.

Build on what students know. Demonstrate the concept; model the concept/procedure. Place student-generated knowledge within conceptual framework.

Scaffolding Activities

1. As children share their knowledge, teacher confirms or expands their knowledge by using pictures of sea animals protecting themselves. Vocabulary is introduced.

2. In small groups with teacher direction, children role-play *some* of the various forms of protection:

    a. poison (e. g., sea anemone)

    b. biting (e. g., barracuda)

    c. tricks (e. g., octopus)

    d. pinching (e. g., crab)

    e. hiding (e. g., reef fish)

    f. swimming (e. g., dolphins)

    g. size (e. g., whales)

    h. electricity (e.g., eel)

    i. talk (e. g., dolphins)

3. Children draw a picture of their favorite sea creature and then tell about its form of protection as they place the picture on a large chart (in child-created categories). Teacher labels categories.

Students engage in scaffolding activities.
Teacher directed

Student directed

Session 2

Focus students' reading. Students use what they already know and the concrete activities to make *predictions* about text materials.	*Review* forms of protection using categorized chart as well as pictures from books (for reinforcement and visualization).	
	Reading in Content Area Teacher introduces book, *Swimmy*, by Leo Lionni. Children are asked to predict the sea animals and the forms of defense that may be found in the book.	Students *read* with teacher to confirm predictions.
	Teacher reads book and then discusses predictions with children to confirm or modify knowledge.	
Discover areas of student confusion. Use small groups so student can discuss what is clear; what isn't.	Children pair with a partner to discuss what is clear; what isn't. Teacher floats around the groups responding to any questions.	Students *collaborate* with each other using exploratory talk.
	and/or	
Use think/write log so students can write what is clear; what isn't.	Teacher gives children think/write log question: "Draw a sea animal and tell about the way it protects itself." Children draw/write in logs. Teacher responds (in written form on log) by commenting (statement or question) on idea(s) in log.	Students *collaborate* with instructor using *expressive writing*.

BIBLIOGRAPHY

Applebee, A. 1981. *Writing in the Secondary School*. Urbana, Ill.: National Council of Teachers of English.

Atwell, N. 1987. *In the Middle: Writing, Reading, and Learning with Adolescents*. Portsmouth, N.H.: Boynton/Cook.

Barnes, D. 1976. *From Communication to Curriculum*. Harmondsworth: Penguin.

Barnes, D.; Britton, J.; and Rosen, H. 1975. *Language, the Learner and the School*. Harmondsworth: Penguin.

Barnes, D., and Todd, F. 1978. *Communication and Learning in Small Groups*. London: Routledge & Kegan Paul.

Barr, M. and Healy, M. K., eds. *What's Going On?* Montclair, N.J.: Boynton/Cook.

Bayer, A. 1977. No Remedial Reading Classes. *California English* 16–17.

———. 1984. Teachers Talking to Learn. *Language Arts* 61:131–139.

———. 1985. On Becoming Teacher Experts: Learning Through Interaction. *Language Arts* 62:412–420.

———. 1986. A Case Study: Teachers' Learning and Language Development. *Journal of Research and Development in Education* 19:19–28.

Britton, J. 1970. *Language and Learning*. Harmondsworth: Penguin.

Britton, J.; Burgress, T.; Martin, N.; McLeod, A.; Rosen, H.   1975. *The Development of Writing Abilities*. London: Macmillan.

Brown, A., and Ferrara, R. 1985. Diagnosing Zones of Proximal Development. In *Cultural Communication and Cognition*. Cambridge: Cambridge University Press.

Bruffee, K. 1983. Writing and Reading as Collaborative or Social Acts: The Argument from Kuhn and Vygotsky. In *The Writer's Mind: Writing as a Mode of Thinking*, edited by J. N. Hays et al. Urbana, Ill.: National Council of Teachers of English.

———. 1984. Collaborative Learning and "The Conversation of Mankind." *College English* 46:635–652.

Bruner, J. 1978. The Role of Dialogue in Language Acquisition. In *The Child's Concept of Language*, edited by A. Sinclair, et al. New York: Springer-Verlag.

———. 1986. *Actual Minds, Possible Worlds*. Cambridge, Mass.: Harvard University Press.

———. 1987. *Making Sense: The Child's Construction of the World*. London and New York: Methuen.

Cohen, E. G. 1986. *Designing Group-Work Strategies for the Heterogeneous Classroom*. New York: Teachers College Press.

Elbow, P. 1981. *Writing With Power*. New York: Oxford University Press.

Forman, E. A., and Cazden, C. B. 1985. Exploring Vygotskian Perspectives in Education: The Cognitive Value of Peer Interaction. In *Culture, Communication and Cognition: Vygotskian Perspectives*, edited by J. V. Wertsch. New York: Cambridge University Press.

Fulwiler, T. 1987. *Teaching With Writing*. Montclair, N.J.: Boynton/Cook.

Goodlad, J. I. 1983. A Study of Schooling: Some Findings and Hypotheses. *Phi Delta Kappan* 64:465–470.

———. 1984. *A Place Called School: Prospects for the Future*. New York: McGraw-Hill.

Goodman, K. S. 1986. *What's Whole in Whole Language?* Portsmouth, N.H.: Heinemann.

Goodman, Y., and Burke, C. 1972. *Reading Miscue Inventory Complete Kit: Procedure for Diagnosis and Evaluation*. New York: Macmillan.

Graves, D. H. 1983. *Writing: Teachers and Children at Work*. Portsmouth, N.H.: Heinemann.

Hallenan, M. 1984. Summary and Implications. In *The Social Contexts of Instruction: Group Organization and Group Process*, edited by L. C. Peterson et al. New York: Academic Press.

Harste, J.; Woodward, V. A.; and Burke, C. L. 1984. *Language Stories and Literacy Lessons*. Portsmouth, N.H.: Heinemann.

Inagaki, K. 1981. Facilitation of Knowledge Integration through Classroom Discussion. *Quarterly Newsletter of the Laboratory of Comparative Human Cognition* 3:26–28.

Inagaki, K., and Hatano, G. 1977. Amplification of Cognitive Motivation and Its Effects on Epistemic Observation. *American Educational Research Journal* 14:485–491.

Johnson, D. W., and Johnson, R. T. 1979. Conflict in the Classroom: Controversy and Learning. *Review of Educational Research* 49:51–70.

Leonard, B. 1982. Prediction Guides: A Subject Area Teacher's Best Friend. *Method: Alaskan Perspectives* 4:29–34.

Lionni, L. 1963. *Swimmy*. New York, N.Y.: Pantheon.

Macrorie, K. 1980. *Searching Writing*. Rochelle, N.J.: Hayden.

———. 1984. *Writing to Be Read*. 3d ed. Montclair, N.J.: Boynton/Cook.

———. 1985. *Telling Writing*. 4th ed. Montclair, N.J.: Boynton/Cook.

Martin, N., et al. 1984. *Writing Across the Curriculum Pamphlets 11–16*. Montclair, N.J.: Boynton/Cook.

Mayher, J. S.; Lester, N.; and Pradl, G. M. 1983. *Learning to Write/Writing to Learn*. Montclair, N.J.: Boynton/Cook.

Mead, G. H. 1934. *Mind, Self and Society*. Chicago: University of Chicago Press.

Moffett, J. 1981. *Active Voice: A Writing Program Across the Curriculum*. Montclair, N.J.: Boynton/Cook.

Newman, J., ed. 1985. *Whole Language: Theory in Use*. Portsmouth, N.H.: Heinemann.

Nicholas, J. 1983. Using Prediction to Increase Content Area Interest and Understanding. *Journal of Reading* 225–228.

Parker, R. P., and Goodkin, V. 1987. *The Consequences of Writing: Enhancing Learning in the Disciplines*. Montclair, N.J.: Boynton/Cook.

Perret-Clermont, A. N. 1980. *Social Interaction and Cognitive Development in Children*. New York: Academic Press.

Richards, J. 1978. *Classroom Language: What Sort?* London: George Allen and Unwin.

Smith, F. 1975. The Role of Prediction in Reading. *Elementary English* 52:305–311.

———. 1985. *Reading Without Nonsense*. New York: Teachers College Press.

———. 1986. *Insult to Intelligence*. New York: Arbor House.

Spear, K. 1988. *Sharing Writing: Peer Response Groups in English Classes.* Portsmouth, N.H.: Boynton/Cook.

Vygotsky, L. S. 1962. *Thought and Language.* Cambridge, Mass.: MIT Press.

———. 1978. In *Mind in Society,* edited by M. Cole, S. Scribner, V. J. Steiner, and E. Souberman. Cambridge, Mass.: Harvard University Press.

Weaver, C. 1988. *Reading Process and Practice: From Sociopsycholinguistics to Whole Language.* Portsmouth, N.H.: Heinemann.

Wertsch, J. V., ed. 1985. *Culture, Communication and Cognition: Vygotskian Perspectives.*Cambridge: Cambridge University Press.

Zemelman, S., and Daniels, H. 1988. *A Community of Writers.* Portsmouth, N.H.: Heinemann.

INDEX